The Elements of News Writing

Third Edition

JAMES W. KERSHNER

Cape Cod Community College

Allyn & Bacon

Boston   Columbus   Indianapolis   New York   San Francisco   Upper Saddle River
Amsterdam   Cape Town   Dubai   London   Madrid   Milan   Munich   Paris   Montréal   Toronto
Delhi   Mexico City   São Paulo   Sydney   Hong Kong   Seoul   Singapore   Taipei   Tokyo

Editor-in-Chief, Communication: Karon Bowers
Senior Acquisitions Editor: Jeanne Zalesky
Editorial Assistant: Stephanie Chaisson
Associate Managing Editor: Bayani Mendoza de Leon
Project Manager: Renata Butera
Manufacturing Buyer: Renata Butera
Marketing Manager: Wendy Gordon
Art Director: Jayne Conte
Project Coordination, Text Design, and Electronic Page Makeup: Jerusha Govindakrishnan / PreMediaGlobal
Cover Designer: Bruce Kenselaar
Cover Printer: Courier/Stoughton

Library of Congress Cataloging-in-Publication Data

Kershner, James W. (James Williamson)
   The elements of news writing / James W. Kershner.—3rd ed.
     p. cm.
   Includes index.
   ISBN-13: 978-0-205-78112-6
   ISBN-10: 0-205-78112-8
  1. Journalism—Authorship.   2. Reporters and reporting.   I. Title.
   PN4775.K37 2011
   808'.06607—dc22

                                  2010050280

4 5 6 7 8 9 10-V092-13 12

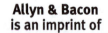

Allyn & Bacon
is an imprint of

www.pearsonhighered.com

ISBN-10:   0-205-78112-8
ISBN-13: 978-0-205-78112-6

This book is dedicated to the memory of
William Middleton Sheppard (1924–2002).
A professor of journalism and mass media at Marietta College
from 1961 to 1988, Shep was a great teacher, adviser,
writer, editor, mentor, and friend.

CONTENTS

PREFACE

In a continually evolving industry that has undergone recent fundamental changes, journalists find themselves facing tough times. Now, more than ever before, there is a starving need for good journalism and thus, good journalists. As we enter the second decade of the twenty-first century, the demand for news and the access to news is greater than ever. This slim volume is based on the assumption that readers, viewers, listeners and consumers of the news in any form want to consume information, and they want to do so in a format that is as short, concise and useful as possible.

Almost a century ago William Strunk wrote his famous admonition to "Omit needless words." In revising this text for the third edition, we took Strunk's words to heart. We added new information about the most recent changes in the news media, but kept the overall length as brief as ever by omitting needless words.

NEW TO THIS EDITION

"You're teaching journalism? Why bother?" Anyone who teaches journalism has heard questions like that in recent years.

As Mark Twain once wrote, "The report of my death was an exaggeration." Speculation about Twain's death circulated throughout his community even when it was a completely false statement. Likewise, journalism is not dead, that too is a false statement.

Our society has a great need for dynamic journalists who are able to adapt to the constantly changing ways in which we send and receive information. This new edition of *The Elements of News Writing* fulfills that need with its up-to-date reflection of the latest changes in the world of news, essential for any emerging journalist. Additions, improvements and changes include:

- A **revised and expanded chapter about "The Future of the Mass Media" (Ch. 35)** that includes information about social media, "smart phones," media convergence, blogs, web journalism and podcasts. Students will learn how new technology is affecting the newsroom and they'll pick up tips on how to utilize this technology.

- A **revised and expanded chapter about punctuation (Ch. 9)** addresses the errors and misunderstandings that trip up most of today's journalism students.

- **Updated chapter coverage** includes references to the new variety of media emerging today and the digitalization of older media.

- A new discussion on the rise of **Facebook** analyzes the ways in which **social networking has completely changed how information is communicated**, teaching as aspiring journalists how to effectively utilize social networking in their fields.

- An analysis of the decisions of several major newspapers to cease publication allows students to **fully comprehend the functionality of the newspaper industry** and how the internet played a role in the demise of these publications.

ACKNOWLEDGMENTS

This book could not have been written without the help, assistance, and encouragement of many people. Particularly helpful have been Michele Auclair, Alison Byland, Jessica Byland, Lore Loftfield DeBower, Vee Frye, Barbara Kershner, Dan McCullough, Cindy Pavlos, and Sarah Polito. The author would also like to thank his students, who have been a continuing inspiration.

Information from *The Associated Press Stylebook and Briefing on Media Law,* © 2010 by The Associated Press, is reprinted with the permission of The Associated Press.

The spelling-checker poem "Candidate for A Pullet Surprise" by Jerrold H. Zar is reprinted with the permission of *The Journal of Irreproducible Results.*

The author appreciates the comments of the following reviewers of the manuscript:

Daniel C. Mason, Mansfield University

Mike Dillon, Duquesne University

Bruce E. Johan, University of Nebraska at Omaha

ABOUT THE AUTHOR

James W. Kershner teaches journalism and writing at Cape Cod Community College. In a 30-year newspaper career, he was a staff reporter for *The Providence Journal*, city editor of the Carlisle (Pa.) *Sentinel*, Sunday editor of the *Cape Cod Times* and executive editor of the four weeklies on Cape Cod owned by the Community Newspaper Co. He holds a bachelor's degree from Marietta College and a master's degree in journalism from Penn State University. He also teaches journalism courses as an adjunct faculty member for Suffolk University. Comments, questions and suggestions may be sent to jkershner@capecod.edu.

What Is News?

Before studying news writing, it is important to consider some definitions. A reporter should know the meaning of the terms *news, newspaper, newsprint, news story, media, medium, mass media, news media, magazine, broadcast, broadcast media,* and *journalism.*

1. NEWS IS A TIMELY ACCOUNT OF A RECENT, INTERESTING, AND SIGNIFICANT EVENT

News writing is the craft of writing news. Before beginning, it makes sense to have an understanding of news itself. William Randolph Hearst was quoted as saying that news is anything that makes a reader say, "Gee whiz."

Hearst was an important figure in the history of American journalism. He was one of the most successful and influential newspaper owners in the late nineteenth and early twentieth centuries. Since the time of Hearst, colloquial expressions of surprise have changed, but news remains something that surprises the reader (or listener or viewer).

Most dictionaries define *news* as an account of a recent event or information that was not known previously to the recipient. Within a family, it may be news that the basement is flooded. Within a neighborhood, it may be news that Mrs. Johnson's cat had kittens. For information to qualify as news in a larger context, though, it must be interesting and significant to a larger number of people. Thus, for the purposes of news writing, *news* can be defined as a timely account of a recent, interesting, and significant event.

When the Japanese attacked Pearl Harbor on Dec. 7, 1941, it was news. When terrorists crashed planes into the World Trade Center on Sept. 11, 2001, it was news. When a man in Omaha, Neb., mowed his lawn in 1942, it was not news. When a child in Atlanta, Ga., completed an uneventful day in second grade in 2010, it was not news. Between the extremes of events that obviously change the course of history and events that are mundane and routine, many events occur that are more or less newsworthy.

Whether these events are news or not depends on how recent, interesting, and significant they are. Of course, those three adjectives—*recent, interesting,* and *significant*—are relative terms. They can be interpreted in different ways by different people in different situations. This is why journalists work hard at trying to decide what information is the most newsworthy.

How Recent Is It?

The more recent the event, the more newsworthy it is. This is why television reporters stress live accounts of *breaking news,* which is news occurring at the same time that it is being reported. Daily newspapers stress news that occurred the day before publication. Follow-up stories of a continuing nature usually begin with the most recent developments in a continuing story. For example, a follow-up on a murder investigation might begin, "Police said today they have no new leads in the case of the heiress who was found dead in her beachfront mansion two years ago." Although the killing took place two years ago, a new statement from the police makes the story newsworthy. The more recent an event, the more likely it is that the readers, listeners, or viewers will have not heard the information before.

Sometimes it takes a while for news to reach us from a remote part of the world, so one might hear that an earthquake in a remote part of China occurred several days ago, but the news was just reported today. This sort of delay was much more common in the past.

The delay in obtaining news is the reason for the journalistic term *dateline.* A *dateline* is the name of a city, in all caps, printed at the beginning of a news story. Originally, a dateline included both the name of a city and the date the dispatch was written. In the eighteenth and nineteenth centuries, news could only travel across the Atlantic Ocean by ship, so American newspapers would print news stories written in Europe and dated before a ship carried the news across the ocean. In the twenty-first century, with instantaneous worldwide digital communication, the term *dateline* reminds us of how far we have come.

How Interesting Is It?

Timeliness obviously is one factor that can make an event interesting, but there are many others. People tend to be interested in things that affect them directly. This brings in the factor of proximity. In general, the nearer something is, the more interesting it is. A murder within a few miles of your home is likely to be very interesting to you, whereas a murder occurring thousands of miles away is likely to be less interesting. However, there are exceptions. The murder trial of O. J. Simpson in 1995 was interesting to people far from California because the defendant was a celebrity. Another factor that can make an event interesting is utility. Columns labeled "News You Can Use" are very popular because people tend to be interested in information they can apply to their own lives. This is why people read about developments in health and fitness; they hope to be able to apply the information to improving their own health and fitness.

People also tend to be interested in information about the basic drives that motivate humans. Everyone needs food, clothing, and shelter, and stories about these subjects tend to have some inherent interest. Two other areas that interest most people are the search for spiritual or religious fulfillment and the search for sexual fulfillment. It has been said that those two areas are usually the subject tackled first by any new means of communication. The fifteenth century saw not only the earliest mass printing, the Gutenberg Bible in 1455 but also the earliest printed pornography. That began an effort to control the publication of obscene material that continues to this day.

In a noted obscenity case, Supreme Court Justice Potter Stewart said of obscenity: "I cannot define it, but I know it when I see it." This description also might be applied to the common term *human interest story.* A human interest story usually is made up of such things as compassion, love, and that tension between selfishness and selflessness that we all feel deep inside. When nine Pennsylvania coal miners trapped underground for 77 hours in a flooded mineshaft were rescued in July of 2002, the whole nation breathed a sigh of relief. It is hard to predict what will make a human interest story, but most people accept that there is a shared humanity that unites us all. This is what interests most humans.

How Significant Is It?

Significance is just as hard to pin down as timeliness or interest. The most important question a journalist can ask is, "How will this affect the readers?" Reporters cover politics routinely; part of the reason is that some politicians are celebrities. The real reason that political news is significant, though, is that the actions of political leaders can affect readers directly. A change in political power can mean that the reader will be paying higher or lower taxes or receiving more or less service from the government. News that means a person will be more or less secure in employment or have more or less security or personal safety is significant because it affects that person. Some events are significant because they have historic importance. Although Neil Armstrong's first step on the moon in 1968 may not have affected many people directly on a personal level, it obviously was significant because it was a historic event. Most people believe that it changed the course of human history in the long run.

The word *news,* of course, is the root of two compound words central to journalism, *newspaper* and *newsprint,* and the phrase *news story.*

2. A NEWSPAPER IS A PUBLICATION, USUALLY PRINTED ON NEWSPRINT, PUBLISHED AT REGULAR INTERVALS, TYPICALLY DAILY OR WEEKLY, AND CONTAINING USEFUL INFORMATION, SUCH AS NEWS, COMMENTARY, FEATURE STORIES, AND ADVERTISING

Although a few newspapers ceased publication during the first decade of the twenty-first century, there are still approximately six thousand newspapers around the world, and no two are exactly alike. The variety is one of the greatest strengths of journalism. People in most places have the opportunity to choose among several newspapers. In North America, there usually were competing newspapers in all major cities between 1850 and 1950. After that, economic factors reduced the number of newspapers in any one city. Nevertheless, in the early twenty-first century, residents usually have a choice of a metropolitan newspaper, a local newspaper, and a regional newspaper, plus one or two national newspapers. The main things that all newspapers have in common are that they contain news, they come out regularly, and they are printed on newsprint.

3. NEWSPRINT IS A LOW-GRADE PAPER MADE FROM WOOD PULP USED CHIEFLY FOR NEWSPAPERS

Since newspapers are printed in large quantities and discarded quickly, it would not be cost-effective to print them on high-quality, long-lasting paper. Most newsprint is produced from wood pulp, but since the 1970s, an increasing quantity of newsprint is made from recycled newsprint itself. According to the Newspaper Association of America, the average amount of recycled fiber in the newsprint used by U.S. newspapers and other newsprint consumers increased from 10 percent in 1989 to more than 35 percent in 2010.

4. A NEWS STORY IS A WRITTEN ACCOUNT OF A RECENT, INTERESTING, AND SIGNIFICANT EVENT PRODUCED FOR DISSEMINATION TO LARGE GROUPS OF PEOPLE

Once a reporter has determined that an event or situation is news, he or she still has to turn it into a news story. This involves gathering the information, analyzing and synthesizing it, organizing it, and presenting it in an interesting way. The specific style, content, and format of a news story depend on the content, the circumstances, and the nature of the news medium. News stories can be presented in newspapers, magazines, or on radio, television, the Internet, or other media.

5. MEDIA IS THE PLURAL OF MEDIUM

Although common usage (and some recent dictionaries) accepts use of the word *media* as a singular collective noun, it is helpful to remember its original use as a plural noun. Misuse of the word *media* in the singular comes up in comments such as, "The media is just out to make money." This implies incorrectly that the media is a single, monolithic unit. The truth is that the media—specifically the mass media—are a ragtag assortment of many different news outlets owned by many different people with many different agendas and priorities. If one wished to attribute the same motivation to all of them, proper usage requires a plural verb: "The media **are** just out to make money."

6. A MEDIUM IS AN INTERMEDIATE SUBSTANCE, AGENCY, OR INSTRUMENT THROUGH WHICH A FORCE ACTS OR AN EFFECT IS PRODUCED

The word *medium* is used many ways in the English language. Picture an exotic-looking woman in a turban sitting at a circular table in a darkened room. As the séance begins, everyone holds hands around the table, and the woman begins to report messages from poor deceased Uncle Henry. She reports that Uncle Henry wants you to give lots of money to this woman, who is a medium. She is the intermediary carrying a message between you and your dead uncle.

In an art class students may have an opportunity to experiment with mixed media, such as oil paints, watercolor, pastels, and charcoal. Each of these is a different medium, and each acts as an intermediary, carrying a message between the artist and the viewer of the art.

In the same way, a newspaper, a magazine, a radio or television broadcast, a Web site, and a bulletin board (either physical or virtual) each is a medium. Each medium is an intermediate agent carrying a message from a source to a recipient.

7. MASS MEDIA ARE MEANS OF COMMUNICATION THAT REACH VERY LARGE NUMBERS OF PEOPLE SIMULTANEOUSLY

Although many people use the term *media* to mean "mass media," it is more accurate to describe newspapers, magazines, radio, and television as the mass media. (The World Wide Web and other parts of the Internet can be considered mass media too.)

8. NEWS MEDIA ARE MEANS OF COMMUNICATION THAT SEND NEWS TO VERY LARGE NUMBERS OF PEOPLE SIMULTANEOUSLY

Mass media are part of the news media to the extent that they carry news. Some media have the ability to transmit news but choose to do very little of that, so it would not be accurate to consider them part of the news media. Examples include radio stations that broadcast only music, television stations that are devoted to home shopping, and periodicals such as comic books. These are part of the mass media but not the news media.

9. A MAGAZINE IS A PUBLICATION ISSUED PERIODICALLY, BOUND IN A PAPER COVER, AND TYPICALLY CONTAINING ARTICLES, STORIES, ESSAYS, POEMS, AND SO ON BY MANY WRITERS AND USUALLY INCLUDING PHOTOGRAPHS, ILLUSTRATIONS, AND ADVERTISING

A magazine, like a newspaper, is a *periodical,* which means that it is published periodically. And like newspapers, magazines contain a variety of useful and interesting information. Magazines usually are distributed weekly, monthly, or quarterly. They are usually printed on higher-quality paper than newsprint.

There are exceptions in both fields, but generally, magazines are likely to appeal to a widely distributed group of people with similar subject-area interests, whereas newspapers are more likely to appeal to a general-interest audience in a more limited geographic area. Newspapers tend to emphasize more timely news, whereas magazines may emphasize less time-sensitive information, including fiction and poetry. By extension, some television programs are described as "magazines" to indicate that they include contents similar to those found in printed magazines.

10. TO BROADCAST IS TO SCATTER OR DISSEMINATE SOMETHING WIDELY

The original meaning of *broadcast* was to "cast broadly," as in sprinkling seed across a field. This image was used to describe the way radio signals (and later television signals) were sent out through the air across a wide geographic area. Radio and television became known as *broadcast media.*

11. BROADCAST MEDIA (SUCH AS RADIO AND TELEVISION) ARE ENTERPRISES THAT TRANSMIT INFORMATION, INCLUDING ENTERTAINMENT, NEWS, AND ADVERTISING, BY SENDING ELECTROMAGNETIC WAVES OVER LARGE AREAS

The term *broadcast media* dates back to the early days of radio in the 1920s, and technology has been changing ever since. In the 1940s, television appeared; in the 1960s, FM broadcasting became popular. In the 1980s, cable television spread throughout most of America. In the late 1990s, satellites became increasingly popular as a means of delivering television and then radio. Digital technology is also changing the means of delivery, but media that are distributed to a large number of home receivers without first being printed on paper are likely to be referred to as *broadcast media* for years to come, even if the signals are not literally "broadcast."

12. JOURNALISM IS THE OCCUPATION OF REPORTING, WRITING, EDITING, PHOTOGRAPHING, PUBLISHING, OR BROADCASTING NEWS

It is worth noting that the English words *journalism* and *journal* both come from the Latin word *diurnal,* meaning "daily." A journal is a daily diary. But the words *journalism* and *journalist* have taken on the added aspects of newsworthiness. The origin of the word underscores the importance of timeliness in journalism.

History of Journalism in the United States

1. IN SOME SENSES, JOURNALISM IS AS OLD AS HUMANKIND

The origins of journalism are lost in antiquity. Surely, when the first cave people huddled around a fire and one of them got too close, that person must have grunted and gestured to let the others know that fire can burn. That was news—a timely account of a recent significant event. But it was only distributed to those within earshot of that first reporter.

Archaeologists have discovered cave paintings that are about 30,000 years old. Some depict hunting scenes. That account of a news event was visible to anyone who visited the cave, so perhaps that was the first mass-media news account.

Anthropologists date the beginning of modern writing to the Sumerian cuneiform writing language of about 3400 B.C.E., or more than 5,000 years ago. That made it much easier to pass along news to a broader audience—at least to anyone who could read.

One well-documented example of a daily posting of written news took place in Ancient Rome. It was known as *Acta Diurna,* or "daily acts." These were accounts of military and political news that were controlled by the government. They were posted in a public square and changed daily.

2. PRINTING MADE THE MASS MEDIA POSSIBLE AND ALSO RAISED THE CONCERN OF RULERS

The first major revolution in journalism was the invention of printing. In China, wood-block printing developed about 1000 C.E., and in Europe, Johannes Gutenberg invented the printing press with movable type in 1440.

Soon there were printers all over Europe. By 1534, King Henry VIII of England required that printers be licensed in order to maintain control of such a powerful technology.

In 1644, the highly respected English author and poet John Milton published an essay titled "Aeropagetica," which was an eloquent plea for freedom of the press. He argued that if truth and falsehood are both given freedom of expression, the truth will win out in the end. This influenced the framers of the American Constitution 140 years later.

The publication most historians consider the first successful newspaper in the English language was published in 1702 by a woman, Elizabeth Mallet.

3. THE FREE PRESS BEGAN IN AMERICA

Although European newspapers had some degree of freedom, it was in America that the truly free press was born.

The first American newspaper was called *Publick Occurances Both Foreign and Domestic.* It was published by Benjamin Harris in 1690 in Boston, but it was short-lived. A more successful newspaper was the *Boston Newsletter,* first published in 1704.

One of the first newspapers to be published without official permission was the *New England Courant,* first published in 1721 by James Franklin. His younger brother, Benjamin Franklin, worked for James as an indentured servant. Ben was supposed to just set type, but writing under the assumed name Silence Dogood, Benjamin Franklin wrote a satirical column that made the paper very popular with its readers. It also drew the ire of colonial officials, and James Franklin was jailed for printing things to which the governor objected. In order to escape the political persecution of the Massachusetts officials and the personal persecution of his older brother, Benjamin Franklin fled to Philadelphia, where he became a successful printer, writer, scientist, inventor, diplomat, and the father of American journalism.

Benjamin Franklin was respected by the founding fathers and, together with Thomas Jefferson, John Adams, and James Madison, ensured the inclusion of freedom of the press in the First Amendment to the Constitution: "Congress shall make no law . . . abridging the freedom of speech, or of the press."

4. THE PARTISAN PRESS FLOURISHED FROM THE 1770S TO THE 1830S

In the early days of the United States, most newspapers were unrestrained in support of a cause or political party. Many newspapers had names such as *The Republican, The Democrat,* or *The Whig.* News was obviously slanted and selected to support the paper's point of view. There also were newspapers of commerce, devoted to printing commercial news for leaders of business. Most cities had a variety of newspapers with various points of view. Magazines also tended to be political. Although papers carried some paid advertising, the subscription price of the publications brought in most of the revenue. The newspapers were comparatively expensive, costing about 3 to 6 cents per issue, which was more than most people could afford.

5. THE PENNY PRESS REPLACED THE PARTISAN PRESS IN THE 1830S

In 1833, Benjamin Day founded the *New York Sun.* Instead of charging more for his newspaper, Day relied on selling more copies at a lower price. He sold his paper for only 1 cent; it was a profitable strategy.

Others followed suit. These papers relied on advertising and mass circulation for their revenue. The sharply partisan tone of their predecessors was not appropriate because that would limit them to people with only that point of view. Papers began to get less partisan and more objective.

6. THE INVERTED-PYRAMID STYLE OF NEWS WRITING BEGAN DURING THE CIVIL WAR

During the Civil War in the 1860s, people were eager to read the latest reports of the war. Reporters took advantage of a new invention, the telegraph, to transmit their stories from the scenes of battles to their home offices. But the telegraph lines were undependable because they kept breaking, either from natural causes or from sabotage. Editors became frustrated when the transmission of a story was interrupted before the reporter even mentioned who won the battle. Orders went out to reporters to be sure to include the most important news in the first paragraph and to put the other details in decreasing order of importance. In that way, if the telegraph transmission were interrupted, at least the most important information would make it. This was the beginning of the inverted-pyramid style of news writing (see Chapter 15).

The Civil War period also marked one of the first early high points of the continuing struggle over censorship and freedom of information. Military commanders attempted to monitor all telegraph communication and censor any news reports that could aid the enemy. President Lincoln is quoted as asking, "Should I hang a soldier for treason and then let editors walk free whose words serve to further rebellion?"

7. YELLOW JOURNALISM BEGAN IN THE 1880S

By the 1880s, advertising was the dominant moneymaker for newspapers, and higher circulation meant more advertising. The battle for circulation heated up, particularly in New York, where William Randolph Hearst's *New York Journal* was in fierce competition with Joseph Pulitzer's *New York World*. In 1895, Pulitzer hired a cartoonist to draw a comic strip that included a character whose long nightshirt was colored yellow. It was the first use of color in printing a newspaper, so it made quite a splash. Soon Hearst and Pulitzer had rival "yellow kids." Meanwhile, both editors favored large headlines designed to appeal to readers' emotions. This new sensationalist style of reporting became known as *yellow journalism.*

In 1898, Hearst and Pulitzer both seemed to be pushing for war with Spain. Hearst sent artist Frederic Remington to Cuba to send back pictures of the war. According to a popular story that historians have not been able to confirm, Remington is supposed to have sent a telegraph saying, "Hate to spend your money. There is no war." And Hearst is said to have replied, "You supply the pictures. I'll supply the war." Soon after that, the U.S. battleship *Maine* was blown up in Havana harbor. Nobody knows what caused the explosion, but the explosion caused the start of the Spanish-American War.

8. CHANGES IN TECHNOLOGY AFFECTED CHARACTERISTICS OF JOURNALISM

Around 1900, several technological changes began affecting journalism. The telegraph had been in use since the 1840s, and newspapers were struggling with how to use it. The first meeting of what was to become the Associated Press (AP) was held in 1848 in an attempt to save money on telegraph costs by sharing resources among six New York newspapers. To get the latest news from Europe, many newspapers sent reporters to Halifax, Nova Scotia, to meet trans-Atlantic steamships, which stopped in Halifax to refuel before arriving in Boston or New York. Rather than every New York newspaper having a correspondent in Halifax, why not share the cost and share the news? The cooperative arrangement was rocky at first, and it was not until 1900 that the AP was formally incorporated as a not-for-profit cooperative.

The idea of newspapers cooperating in a "wire service" meant that correspondents had to write in a style that would be acceptable to a variety of clients. Since it couldn't be slanted to please one or two editors, wire-service stories emphasized just the facts, with little interpretation or slant.

Like telegraphy, photography had been around since the 1840s. It gained prominence in the Civil War and began to be used commonly in newspapers around 1900.

Another new technology was the invention of the Linotype machine by Ottmar Mergenthaler in 1885. This machine casts type one whole line at a time out of hot lead. Before that, lines of type were assembled by piecing together pieces of type representing individual letters. The Linotype made it possible to produce newspapers much more quickly.

Sadly, author Samuel Clemens (Mark Twain)—who had begun his writing career as a newspaper reporter—invested a fortune in a competing machine that lost out to the Linotype, leaving Clemens impoverished.

9. RADIO AND TELEVISION CHANGED JOURNALISM BUT DID NOT REPLACE NEWSPAPERS

Technology continued to change newspapers, mostly by speeding up the newsgathering process, throughout the twentieth century. In 1903, Guglielmo Marconi transmitted radio waves across the Atlantic, beginning the use of radio waves for long-distance communication and laying the framework for popular use of radio as a means of mass communication. By the 1920s, most homes in America had radio receivers.

Television came soon after that. By 1960, most American homes had television receivers. Television and radio altered the face of journalism worldwide. As each of these mass media emerged, people predicted that they would replace newspapers, but that did not happen. People continued to read newspapers at roughly the same rate as before the popularity of the broadcast media developed.

In the early 1960s, offset printing sped up the process of printing newspapers and was followed by "cold type" typesetting, which replaced the old "hot type" Linotype machines with a phototypesetting process that created a plate of each page based on an original page created without the use of any lead type at all.

10. THE ASSASSINATION OF PRESIDENT JOHN F. KENNEDY CHANGED TELEVISION JOURNALISM FOREVER

On Nov. 22, 1963, Dan Rather was working for a local CBS affiliate in Dallas and was asked to deliver a large tin containing film to a station across town. That's when he witnessed chaos and confusion in the street around Dealey Plaza and headed for the hospital, where he heard from a priest that the president had been assassinated. Rather fed the information to Walter Cronkite, who was the anchor of the "CBS Evening News." Millions of Americans learned of Kennedy's death from Cronkite, rather than from a daily newspaper.

It was a story that changed the character of television journalism. Until that time, television news was largely confined to 15- or 30-minute news broadcasts with an occasional special report. But Kennedy's assassination was such a big story that the networks preempted all regular programming and stayed on the air around the clock. Viewers stayed glued to their television sets watching the drama unfold before their eyes.

Before the end of the twentieth century, there were several cable networks offering round-the-clock news reports.

11. DIGITALIZATION OF INFORMATION BEGINNING IN THE 1970S REVOLUTIONIZED THE MASS MEDIA AGAIN

The last third of the twentieth century has been called the information age. The basic change, in terms of journalism, is that words could be stored in digital form on magnetic tape or computer disks.

Some newspapers began using digital storage of information in the 1970s. The personal computer became common in the 1980s, and soon newspapers converted from large mainframe computers to networks of personal computers. The Internet changed from a small academic curiosity to a popular institution in the 1990s. Almost every newspaper, television station, and radio station developed a Web site in the mid-1990s.

As with radio and television, there were predictions that the Internet would replace newspapers, but that has failed to come true. People seem to cling to the old-fashioned concept of a medium printed on paper that they can hold in their hands and carry around easily.

In the late 1990s, most newspapers began using digital photography instead of exposing images on light-sensitive film. Digital words and images could be stored on computers and made up into pages without ever printing anything on paper, further speeding the newspaper production process.

At the dawn of the twenty-first century, new technology came fast and furious. Reporters anywhere in the world could send digital video signals over a satellite phone that could be presented on live television or a Web site or converted to still pictures and printed in newspapers. Some newspapers were offering customized versions of their papers delivered in different forms to different people's computer terminals or cellular phones. People with access to the Internet could gain instant access to virtually unlimited information.

12. THROUGHOUT HISTORY, THREE COMMON THREADS EMERGE: PEOPLE STRUGGLE TO CONTROL INFORMATION, TECHNOLOGY CHANGES THE WAY INFORMATION IS TRANSFERRED, AND THE NEED FOR JOURNALISTS CONTINUES

As long as people have exchanged information, there has been a feeling that knowledge is power. This is why people have tried to control information. The history of journalism is rife with examples of journalists trying to disseminate information and officials trying to keep secrets. In recent years, state and federal "freedom of information" laws have been passed in the United States to try to keep information open, but the struggle continues.

Meanwhile, from the days of assembling pieces of type by hand to the days of imbedded reporters broadcasting news live, technology has contributed to the increasing speed of news delivery. Back in 1814, the Treaty of Ghent was signed on Dec. 24, ending the War of 1812, but word did not reach the troops in the field in time to stop the Battle of New Orleans on Jan. 8, 1815. In 2003, the Battle of Baghdad was watched live on millions of TV sets. The technology itself has changed, but the fact that new means of communication are being developed every day has remained constant in journalism.

The biggest constant factor in the history of journalism is the continuing need for journalists. No change in technology has replaced the need for an intelligent, sensitive, knowledgeable person to ask questions; to gather information; to synthesize, analyze, and organize it; and then to present the news in a clear way. Whether people are reading the news on a cave wall or on a handheld computer, someone will have to find out what is happening and let others know about it. This is the essence of news writing.

In April of 1995, writing coach Don Fry of the Poynter Institute presented a program at the National Writers Workshop in Hartford, Conn., about the future of newspapers. He predicted that within a decade or so there would be customized digital newspapers that people would receive on palm-sized receivers.

I told my journalism students about his prediction, but I retained some healthy skepticism. Then in 1998 I was reading the Christian Science Monitor and saw an announcement headlined, "Customized news available via *Monitor.*" Just as Don Fry predicted, subscribers could enter their preferences and receive a digital newspaper with the types of news in which they were interested. But most people would still receive this on a full-sized desktop computer, I figured. The following year, in December 1999, the media journal *Brill's Content* featured the top 10 content tools of 1999, and there at number five was the Palm VII by PalmPilot, described as the first personal digital assistant (PDA) that lets you surf Web sites from your electronic organizer. Don Fry's prediction had come true in only four years.

I continued to tell this story to my classes, and they soon had trouble understanding how outlandish Fry's predictions sounded in 1995. Then one day, in the spring of 2003, I told the story, and at the end, when I mentioned PDAs with wireless Internet connections, a young man in the back row—Michael Cordry—raised his hand, "You mean like this?" he asked, holding up his PDA.

There was Don Fry's outlandish science-fiction prediction right in the back row of my classroom.

The Role of the News Media in American Society

1. THE NEWS MEDIA KEEP PEOPLE INFORMED

People rely on the news media to learn about events in their world. Even people who do not read newspapers or catch the news on radio, television, or the Internet will hear about news because a friend of theirs will have learned about it from the news media. People frequently begin conversations with questions such as, "Did you hear about the space shuttle?" or "Did you hear about the big fire?" or "Did you hear what the president said?" These questions usually are followed by an explanation that, "It was in the paper," or "I saw it on TV," or "It was all over the Internet."

2. THE NEWS MEDIA MAKE US A COMMUNITY

When the twin towers fell, when the first man walked on the moon, when President Kennedy was assassinated, we knew about it because of the mass media. In each of those examples, we all knew about it at once; it was a shared experience.

In the case of national tragedies, the news media also tell us about memorial services and other efforts to express national grief. The shared outpouring of emotions builds a sense of community. After the Sept. 11 tragedy, people gathered all over the world to express their grief. When the television networks in the United States broadcast the scene of thousands of Canadians gathering outside the Parliament Building in Ottawa to express their sympathy, it created a sense of North American community that affected people all over North America. Such community building happens on an international, national, and local level.

Earlier in history, our society shared other common experiences, although not simultaneously. The Declaration of Independence, the Emancipation Proclamation, and completion of the Transcontinental Railroad were reported in the mass media of their times, and our society shared those experiences too.

3. THE NEWS MEDIA PROVIDE PEOPLE WITH INFORMATION THEY NEED TO PARTICIPATE IN A DEMOCRACY

Democracy is rule by the people, so it is logical that people need to participate in the government. For this to work effectively, people need information about the issues of the day. They need to know when elections are scheduled and who is running for office. They need to know the positions of the candidates. People also need to know about meetings of local, state, regional, and national governing bodies. The news media play a vital role in providing this information to the public.

For example, in Barnstable, Mass., in 2003, the local news media, including a daily newspaper, three weekly newspapers, and several radio stations, reported that the town council was planning to approve the construction of an affordable housing development. Soon people were debating it, and the newspapers printed letters to the editor both for and against the plan. Then the local media reported that an independent water district with its own governing board wanted to purchase the same land for watershed protection, effectively killing the housing plan. But the district was required to hold a public hearing. Because of the news stories, hundreds of people crowded into the hearing room, causing the water board to reschedule the hearing and move it to a larger hall. Little dramas like this are played out all over the United States every day because local news media provide information about actions of local governments.

4. THE NEWS MEDIA PROVIDE A CHECK ON THE POWER OF GOVERNMENT

Watergate, the Pentagon Papers, the Iran-Contra scandal—there have been numerous recent episodes in which an aggressive press corps has exposed wrongdoing on the part of the government. Pulitzer Prize-winning investigative journalist Seymour Hersh uncovered the My Lai massacre during the Vietnam War in 1969 and then the Abu Graib prison scandal during the Iraq War in 2004. But the tradition goes back much farther than those cases. Famous "muckrakers" such as Lincoln Steffens and Upton Sinclair exposed wrongdoing at the beginning of the twentieth century, and Thomas Paine's *Common Sense* is cited by many as a major cause of the American Revolution.

5. THE NEWS MEDIA PLAY A VITAL ROLE IN BUSINESS AND COMMERCE

The news media are important to commercial business in two ways. First, most news media are supported by advertising, and those advertisements are the primary means most businesses have of telling the public about their products and services. These include everything from full-page color advertisements in news magazines announcing the introduction of a new car model to a small classified ad in a local newspaper placed by an individual selling a used car. Consumers often peruse the advertising in a newspaper or magazine to learn what is available and to compare products.

A second way the news media contribute to business and commerce is through business reporting. Most newspapers, news magazines, and broadcast news operations recognize the need to report on business activities. Mergers, layoffs, new products, and feature stories about interesting successes and failures are all grist for the business-reporting mill.

Of course, it is also true that the news media are themselves businesses. They employ large numbers of people, buy and sell products, and participate in the economic life of a community. In a small town, for example, the local newspaper is likely to buy or lease a fleet of delivery trucks from a local car dealership and buy fuel from a local service station. Factors such as these also affect an area's economy.

6. THE NEWS MEDIA PROVIDE A FORUM FOR THE EXCHANGE OF OPINIONS AND DEVELOPMENT OF CONSENSUS

Most newspapers and magazines include letters to the editor and op/ed columns that provide for an exchange of opinions about controversial subjects (see Chapter 22). Readers are likely to read those expressions of opinion and think about whether they agree or disagree with the views. Readership studies consistently indicate that letters to the editor are among the most popular features of newspapers. Most newspaper Web sites also include means for readers to express their opinions.

7. THE NEWS MEDIA PROVIDE A ROUGH DRAFT OF HISTORY

Philip L. Graham (1915–1963), longtime publisher of the *Washington Post,* once said that journalism is "the first rough draft of history." News writers inform people of recent significant events in a timely fashion, but their reports are used for many years thereafter by researchers interested in what happened in the past. Historians and magazine fact-checkers routinely use old newspapers to confirm what was happening in the past.

8. THE NEWS MEDIA PROVIDE PEOPLE WITH HELPFUL, PRACTICAL INFORMATION

Is it going to rain tomorrow? When does the town dump open? When are the Fourth of July fireworks going to begin? For answers to questions such as these, millions of readers turn to their newspapers. In recent years, more and more people have begun using the Internet to get such information, but many still find their newspaper a more convenient way to learn about such things.

Furthermore, the news media often include practical information alongside traditional news. There may be recipes, fitness tips, consumer information, movie and television guides, fashion tips, and health news. Advice columns include such diverse topics as how to reduce utility bills, how to care for a pet, and how to repair a car.

9. THE NEWS MEDIA SATISFY PEOPLE'S SENSE OF CURIOSITY

There are items in the news media that people find fascinating despite the fact that they may not have great significance or a direct impact on their lives. For example, Springfield, Mass., and Battle Creek, Mich., regularly compete for the honor of hosting the world's largest breakfast. Certain movie stars appear to be in a competition to see who can get married and divorced the most times. And every few years someone receives a letter that was mailed decades earlier and misplaced en route. Nobody would go looking for these stories, but people seem to be curious about them.

Parade magazine, the Sunday supplement that is distributed in more than 500 Sunday newspapers, has tapped into the curiosity factor with its annual feature entitled, "What People Earn." It publishes the salary of dozens of people from all walks of life.

10. THE NEWS MEDIA ENTERTAIN PEOPLE

From the time of Benjamin Franklin's Silence Dogood columns to today's Web logs, or "blogs," the news media have included entertainment. Humor columns, comic strips, horoscopes, funny photographs, and celebrity interviews are part of the news media because they entertain people.

Sports reporting is a special category of news that many consider a form of entertainment. Although some of it is news, it is news about an enterprise that is basically entertainment. The same can be said of news about the entertainment industry in general, including radio, television, film, and the fine arts.

In recent years, newspapers and television news shows have struggled to hold onto their readership and viewership, and some have tried to appeal to more people by making their news more entertaining. Celebrity news and lighthearted feature stories are more and more common. Some critics dismiss this as "infotainment," and lament the decrease in hard-hitting investigative reporting.

The Daily Show with Jon Stewart, which premiered in 1996, is a comedy news show based on political satire. It is much more popular among people under 30 than are the traditional news shows. Jon Stewart himself has been quoted many times as lamenting the fact that many members of his audience use his show as their only source of news. The growing popularity of YouTube and other Internet entertainment sites in 2006 and 2007 indicate a blurring of the traditional distinction between news and entertainment. The presidential campaign leading up to the election of 2008 featured debates cosponsored by YouTube and MySpace, and every presidential candidate has a Web presence. Hillary Rodham Clinton made her formal announcement that she was a candidate for president in a video posted on her Web site.

11. THE NEWS MEDIA PLAY A ROLE IN THE EXCHANGE OF INFORMATION ABOUT RELIGION, SPIRITUALITY, AND PHILOSOPHY

General-interest news media usually include some news about religious activities. Local newspapers, for example, usually include a schedule of religious services and an occasional article about news related to religion. There are numerous syndicated columns dealing with religion and spirituality, and some general opinion columns delve into religious topics from time to time. Occasionally, a major news story deals with spiritual themes, such as the national debate about prayer in school, state support of religious schools, and federal aid to faith-based initiatives to help people.

Furthermore, there are scores of religious publications of all sorts. Some are designed to exchange information among members of a specific denomination, some are designed to publish new scholarly research on spiritual topics, and some are designed to proselytize.

One particularly interesting publication is the *Christian Science Monitor,* which is supported by the Christian Science Church but is not a religious publication. It is famous for its editorial independence, objectivity, fairness, and balance. It has won seven Pulitzer Prizes since it was founded in 1908. After 100 years of daily publication, the *Monitor* ceased daily publication in 2008 to focus on a news Web site and weekly magazine.

12. THE NEWS MEDIA PROVIDE AN EFFICIENT MEANS FOR DISTRIBUTION OF INFORMATION IMPORTANT FOR PUBLIC SAFETY

In 1994, the Emergency Alert System replaced the familiar Emergency Broadcast System, which was famous for the familiar phrase, "This is a test of the Emergency Broadcast System. If this had been an actual emergency. . . ." These emergency networks represent the most formal means of distributing emergency information through the mass media, but the news media distribute emergency information in many other ways.

Newspapers report on the approach of hurricanes and the spread of wildfires. Television stations provide live coverage of approaching storms, and radio stations broadcast school closings and locations of shelters in times of emergencies. The news media also co-operate with law-enforcement agencies in asking the public for information about crimes. And in reporting about criminal activities, the media give people information about their relative safety.

13. THE NEWS MEDIA PROVIDE INFORMATION ABOUT THE FINE AND PERFORMING ARTS

The news media routinely provide previews and reviews of art shows, dance recitals, concerts, plays, films, and other performances. Newspapers usually include calendar sections with detailed schedules of performances and exhibits. Occasional feature stories profile artists, musicians, and performers. The public gets most of its information about the arts from the general news media.

There are also specialized media that concentrate on the arts or specific areas of artistic expression. There are newspapers and magazines that focus on such specific areas of artistic expression as performance art, bluegrass music, Irish step dancing, and independent filmmaking.

14. THE NEWS MEDIA PROVIDE A MEANS FOR PEOPLE TO EXCHANGE PERSONAL INFORMATION

Primarily through classified advertising, the news media allow people to exchange information for personal reasons. There are personal ads in which people try to find suitable friends, dates, or mates. There are transportation ads in which people try to find rides or people to drive their cars somewhere. There are ads looking for babysitters or looking for babysitting jobs. And there are lost-and-found ads and ads for items for sale listing everything under the sun.

Before 2000, almost all of these ads appeared in newspapers. But after 2000, classified advertising moved rapidly to free Internet-based sites, primarily Craigslist, which was founded in 1995 and became a major national presence in 2003, when it expanded to listings for 14 cities. In 2010, Craigslist was publishing more than eighty million new classified advertisements each month in more than 700 cities or regions.

15. THE NEWS MEDIA SHOWCASE A VARIETY OF WRITING STYLES

Although the main purpose of the news media is to provide information, the way the information is presented can be interesting itself. Great writers such as Mark Twain and Ernest Hemingway began as newspaper reporters, and wonderful writing appears in the mass media every day. Essays in magazines and columns in newspapers are designed to showcase good writing, but fine writing can be found on radio broadcasts, television features, and even straightforward news stories.

16. THE NEWS MEDIA SHOWCASE A VARIETY OF PHOTOGRAPHY AND GRAPHIC ART

Most newspapers publish news photos, sports photos, feature photos, and other kinds of graphic art every day. Some are informative and practical, and some are spectacularly beautiful. Magazines, especially, tend to concentrate on presenting beautiful photographs. Bringing this art into American homes every day is part of the role of the news media in American society.

17. THE NEWS MEDIA RAISE PEOPLE'S AWARENESS ABOUT SOCIETIES AND CULTURES DIFFERENT FROM THEIR OWN

It is through the news media that Americans learned about the Muslim tradition of women wearing a burka. It was through the news media that Americans learned about the meditative practices of Tibetan Buddhist monks. If the world seems to be getting smaller, it is probably because the news media bring us news from all over the globe instantly.

> In the early 1990s, the *Cape Cod Times* participated in a variety of international exchanges with foreign journalists. In 1991, one visiting journalist was Askar Alamzhanov, who came as a representative of the Union of Soviet Journalists. By the time he returned to his home in Almaty, Kazakhstan, a few weeks later, there was no longer a Union of Soviet Socialist Republics. While he was in the United States, I took him to New York City and we visited Central Park. When we got to Strawberry Fields, the peaceful plaza memorializing John Lennon, I read the inscription in the marble mosaic, and it brought tears to my eyes. Then I looked at Askar, who had lived his whole life in Central Asia, just about as far from New York as one could get on earth. There were tears in his eyes too. The news media in Kazakhstan had reported on the life and death of John Lennon. Two journalists from opposite parts of the earth were both affected the same way by visiting the place where John Lennon had enjoyed sitting in the park playing his guitar.

Kershner's Five Rules of Journalism

The following list is unabashedly simplistic. There is much more to good journalism, of course. When a beginner is working on a news story, however, it may be helpful to refer to these five rules to evaluate the story. The list is designed for people who need a handful of easy-to-remember guidelines. The first letter of each rule creates the mnemonic *RAFTS*. If you are trying to write a news story and feel like you are drowning, grab onto these RAFTS.

1. *Remember the basics.* Tell the reader who, what, where, when, why, and how. Use standard American English spelling, punctuation, and grammar.
2. *Accuracy, accuracy, accuracy!* These are Joseph Pulitzer's three rules of journalism. Make sure that you get it right. Facts, figures, and spellings must be accurate.
3. *Find your focus.* What's the story? What's the point? If you can't say it in 25 words or less, you probably haven't found your focus.
4. *Think short.* Use short words in short sentences in short paragraphs in short stories.
5. *Strive to be objective.* Don't let your opinions or those of the sources get in the way of a straight, objective story. Remember, your main obligation is to the reader, who wants the unvarnished truth. Write what the reader wants to know, which is not necessarily what the source wants to say.

Now let's look at each in greater detail.

1. REMEMBER THE BASICS

What are the basics? In journalism, every beginner starts with the time-tested *five W's*: *who, what, where, when,* and *why*. Most experts add *how* and perhaps *so what* to these. If a news story breaks suddenly and reporters are rushing to the scene, there is little time for them to plan a list of questions, so most will rely on the five W's to get them started in their investigation.

For example, in an automobile accident, the reporter might ask a police officer questions based on the five W's:

"*Who* were the drivers and passengers?"

"*What* was the result—were there injuries or damage?"

"*Where* did it occur?"

"*When*—exactly—did the accident occur?"

"*Why* did it happen—what was the cause?"

Then, after all the reporting, the reporter might use those same questions to structure the story. After the story is written, the reporter should look it over to make sure that all the basic questions are covered. This is one side to covering the basics.

There is another side to remembering the basics, and that side is making sure that the copy is *clean*. In a newsroom, *clean copy* is the term for writing that uses correct spelling, punctuation, grammar, and style. Journalists don't keep their jobs long if they cannot master the basics of proper English. Although news stories are processed by copy editors, no reporter should ever hand in sloppy copy with the attitude that "That's what copy editors are for." Making sure that a news story is free from mistakes is a cooperative job that takes the best efforts of everyone who handles the story—especially the reporter.

2. ACCURACY, ACCURACY, ACCURACY!

According to an old saying in business, the three most important things are "location, location, location." In journalism, the three most important things are "accuracy, accuracy, accuracy." The newsroom aphorism "accuracy, accuracy, accuracy" is usually attributed to Joseph Pulitzer, who, according to several biographers, had the phrase posted on his newsroom wall. Pulitzer was born in Hungary in 1847 and moved to the United States in 1864. He worked on the German-language *Westliche Post* as a reporter, managing editor, and later publisher. In 1883, he moved to New York and bought the *New York World* newspaper. Using a mix of populism, sensationalism, and crusades against corruption, he built it into the largest-circulation newspaper in America. In 1903, he donated $1 million to Columbia University for the establishment of a School of Journalism, which, in turn, established the prestigious Pulitzer Prizes in his honor.

The reason that accuracy is so important is that a newspaper (or other news medium) depends on its credibility. If the readers (or listeners or viewers) do not have faith that the information is accurate, they will not trust it. And if they don't trust the information, they will turn elsewhere for their news.

It is often the simplest little details that cause the biggest problems. If a reporter misspells the name of a person in a feature story, everyone who knows the correct spelling of that person's name will begin to mistrust all the information in the story. If a reporter writes in a story that the capital of Maryland is Baltimore, everyone who knows that the capital is really Annapolis will be tempted to say, "Well, if the reporter got that wrong, what else in this story is incorrect?"

3. FIND YOUR FOCUS

In optics, a *focus* is a single point, not a broad area. The same is true in journalism; a story can have only one point. Yes, a story can contain many supporting details and additional information, but everything has to support one single point. That is the focus. Journalists use various terms to refer to this focus. Often it is simply the *lead* (pronounced "leed"), which is the sentence or paragraph that leads off the story.

A good lead lets the reader know the focus of the story clearly and quickly. News stories do not have introductions that beat around the bush before getting to the main point. Some feature stories may use a quotation or anecdote to heighten interest in the subject, but they still get to the main point quickly.

Another way to define the focus is in a "nut graf," which is newsroom jargon for a paragraph that summarizes the story in a nutshell. Every story should have a "nut graf," which may or may not be the same as the lead. And every story must have a clear focus.

A reporter who says that a story is "about child safety seats and accidents and traffic safety and driving distractions and new laws" is just brainstorming with no focus. If the reporter does some research and determines that the story is "Child safety seats save lives," then the reporter has a good story with a sharp, clear focus.

4. THINK SHORT

In writing, shorter is better. If there is a shorter word with the same meaning as a longer one, use it. If there is a shorter sentence with the same meaning as a longer one, use it. Readers appreciate this.

Walt Whitman wrote: "Write short; to the point; stop when you have done. . . . Read it over again, abridge, and correct it until you get it into the shortest space possible."

Paragraphs in news writing must be shorter than paragraphs in academic or literary writing. Because newspaper columns typically are about 12 picas (or two inches) wide, a long paragraph tends to look daunting to readers. Keeping paragraphs shorter makes stories look more inviting. In broadcast journalism, paragraphs must be short to make them easier for the broadcaster to read and the listener to understand. And on the Internet, short paragraphs are favored for similar reasons. No one likes to read long blocks of type on a computer screen.

5. STRIVE TO BE OBJECTIVE

Can a journalist be truly objective? This question opens the door to a complex debate involving ethics, philosophy, psychology, sociology, and communication theory. While theorists argue the abstract issues involved, working journalists have to live in the real world, where they have to attempt to be as objective as possible despite human conflicts. When readers pick up a newspaper or viewers tune into a newscast, they expect the information to be free of bias or prejudice. This is why good journalists attempt to get all sides of a story. They attempt to be fair to all points of view. They attempt to give enough information so that the readers or viewers can make up their own minds.

There are factors making this difficult. All reporters come to the job with built-in prejudices and biases. They have to consciously avoid letting these influence them. The sources who provide information have another set of biases, and the reporters have to be aware of these and avoid them. The publication itself, its owners or advertisers, may have points of view that could influence coverage. A good reporter at a good publication will guard against being influenced by these factors.

For example, a reporter writing about a protest at a clinic that conducts abortions probably will have his or her own point of view on the controversy. The reporter must think carefully about how to describe people on each side of the issue. Are the people with signs "antiabortion," "right to life," or "pro-life"? Are they "demonstrators," "activists," or "protesters"? And are the people of the other side of the issue "pro-abortion," "abortion-rights," or "pro-choice"? Are the health-care workers "physicians," "abortion doctors," "baby killers," or "reproductive health workers"? Are they standing outside an "abortion clinic," a "women's health facility," or a "healthcare center"?

Reporters must be aware of the loaded language involved and try to find a way to describe the situation as objectively as possible, leaving the conclusions and value judgments up to the readers, listeners, or viewers. Perfect objectivity may be impossible to achieve, but a reporter who strives to achieve it is serving the public well.

In October of 2006 I was invited to present a workshop on "Kershner's Five Rules of Journalism" at the annual convention of College Media Advisers in St. Louis, Mo. It was the same week that the St. Louis Cardinals were in the World Series against the Detroit Tigers. I arrived in St. Louis Friday night, Oct. 27, after a series of delays that meant I missed the reception for advisers. So I stepped out of my hotel and walked up the street looking for a place to eat dinner. I paused outside the open doors of a Hooters restaurant and bar that had a big flat-screen TV showing the opening of the World Series game in Busch Stadium just two blocks behind me. I watched the national anthem and then heard a roar from the crowd coming from the big-screen TV in front of me in the bar. And then, a few seconds later, I heard the real roar from the real crowd in the stadium behind me. I found a quieter place to get a sandwich and then retreated to my hotel room to watch the game on TV. In the ninth inning Cardinals pitcher Adam Wainwright struck out Detroit's Brandon Inge to end the game and give the St. Louis team its first World Series championship in 24 years. The crowd—as the cliché goes—went wild.

Once again, I heard the roar on TV, and then I could hear it through my closed hotel window. I cautiously stepped outside the hotel and got a glimpse of an entire city in a frenzy of celebration. It was impossible not to get swept up in the excitement.

The next morning I ended up spending more time talking about the news value of proximity than anything else. The World Series is a big story anywhere, but the closer you are the bigger it is. And when you are standing close enough to hear the crack of the bat and roar of the jubilant hometown crowd, that makes it bigger still.

Basics of Good Journalism

The five rules of journalism in Chapter 4 are short, simple, and easy to remember, but a good journalist needs to look a little more deeply at the profession. Here are 10 principles that are a little more advanced:

1. REMEMBER THAT YOUR BASIC OBLIGATION IS TO THE READER. JOURNALISTS ARE WORKING FOR THEIR READERS. YOU SHOULD NEVER WRITE SOMETHING JUST BECAUSE A SOURCE WANTS TO SEE IT IN PRINT. AND YOU SHOULD NEVER WRITE SOMETHING JUST BECAUSE YOU WANT TO SEE IT IN PRINT

Journalists may feel like they are working for several bosses. It is only natural to want to please the editor who assigned the story and other editors at the newspaper, including the editor who hired you. And, after interviewing a source for an article, it is common to want to write an article that pleases the source, especially if the source has been helpful and cooperative. Another natural human tendency is the desire to write something that pleases us. Nevertheless, a good journalist will think first and foremost of the reader. In deciding what to include in a story and what to leave out, reporters should ask themselves, "What does the reader need to know?"

Sometimes a source will attempt to dictate the form and content of a news story. A good journalist will resist these efforts politely but firmly. This can be particularly troublesome among student journalists interviewing faculty and staff members at their own school. If this happens, good reporters thank the source for his or her advice and mention that they will be talking to several other sources and that the final decisions about what to include will be made by the newspaper's editor.

Reporters also should resist the temptation to include something in a story just because the reporters themselves would like to see it in print. It may be a particularly well-turned phrase that shows off the writer's skill or a fascinating little tidbit that demonstrates extraordinary depth of research. However, reporters should leave their egos at the newsroom door and run the information through the same filter that is the key to good news writing: Is this something the reader needs to know?

For example, a reporter is working on a story about an upcoming 10K road race. The race organizer may say that it is very important to include the names of several sponsors who contributed goods or financial backing to make the race a success. Although the race organizer may think that it is vital to include this information, do the readers really benefit from knowing it? It is more likely the readers will want to know the date, time, and location of the race. They may want to know how to enter the race, how to watch the race, or how to avoid the traffic jam it will cause. They also may want to know that a 10K race is 10 kilometers long, which is 6.2 miles. It is much less likely that they will be wondering which company supplied the free bottled water given out at the finish line.

2. WHAT'S THE STORY? WHAT'S THE POINT? THESE TWO QUESTIONS CAN HELP YOU TO FIND YOUR FOCUS. IF YOU CANNOT ANSWER THEM QUICKLY AND EASILY, YOU MAY NOT HAVE A STORY. GOOD JOURNALISM CONSISTS OF GOOD STORIES WITH CLEAR POINTS. YOU SHOULD BE ABLE TO STATE THE MAIN POINT OF YOUR STORY IN 25 WORDS OR LESS

At many good newspapers, reporters submit "budget items," which are brief summaries of their stories for use in the news budget that is discussed by editors planning the edition. This is a good exercise in identifying the focus of a story. A reporter must be able to state the main point of the story in a simple declarative sentence. In most cases, this also will be the lead of the story.

Mitchell Stephens, author of *Broadcast News* and professor of journalism at New York University, once said that a reporter should "focus Zen-like on the kernel of the story." If you don't know what the kernel of your story is, try asking yourself, "What's the story?" and "What's the point?"

3. REMEMBER THAT YOU ARE TRYING TO INFORM PEOPLE. THE MAIN PURPOSE OF A NEWSPAPER IS TO INFORM THE PUBLIC. DO NOT LEAVE "HOLES" IN YOUR STORIES WHERE INFORMATION IS MISSING

What time is the concert? Was the driver wearing a seat belt? Did the police arrest anyone? How much did it cost? What is the manager's salary? How much money was stolen? How much will it cost the average taxpayer? All these are questions a good editor might ask after reading stories with "holes" in them. A piece of missing information leaves a hole in a story. A good news story will include all the information the reader is likely to want to know. A good reporter should make every effort to answer all such questions.

Occasionally, as a last resort, a journalist may have to include a note that "police refused to release information" about something or indicate that repeated attempts to contact someone for more information failed. For example, if a reporter is covering a story about a movie being filmed in the paper's town, the reporter will want to get quotes from the stars, the director, and the local extras who are thrilled to be a part of a big

Hollywood film. The reporter may be very excited to get an interview with a big-name star about how much the celebrity enjoyed visiting the reporter's hometown. However, when the story comes out, the readers will be wondering when the film is scheduled for release. If this information is not in the story, readers will be calling the newsroom asking about it. An editor is likely to yell across the newsroom a harsh criticism about how "that story had a hole you could drive a Mack truck through."

4. DON'T WRITE ANYTHING YOU WOULDN'T READ. IF YOU DO NOT FIND IT INTERESTING, YOUR STORY WILL NOT BE READ. IF THERE IS INFORMATION WORTHY OF PRINTING, YOU MUST FIND AN ANGLE THAT MAKES IT INTERESTING TO YOU

Sometimes reporters get "stuck" with a lousy story. The subject seems boring or trivial. If an editor sticks you with one of these "turkeys," should you just hold your nose and write a bad story?

No. In a situation such as this, a good reporter will look for an angle to bring some life or interest to the story. For example, if the assignment is to write a story about the donation of a defibrillator to a fire station, it could result in a boring account of the local civic group donating money to buy the equipment. Even worse, it might be accompanied by the dreaded "grip and grin" photo of the civic group president shaking hands with the fire chief in front of the piece of machinery. With a little digging, though, a good reporter might be able to find the name of a person whose life was saved by the use of a defibrillator. Interviewing that person and some family members could result in an exciting story of a dramatic rescue in a life-and-death situation.

5. HOW WILL THIS AFFECT YOUR READERS? A GOOD REPORTER ALWAYS ASKS THIS QUESTION. THE ANSWER WILL HELP TO IDENTIFY THE LEAD AND DETERMINE HOW NEWSWORTHY THE STORY IS

Although it seems obvious that a reporter should ask how the story affects readers, this is easy to overlook. For example, after covering a municipal meeting in which the officials discuss taxes in terms of "mills," "percentages," or "rate hikes," a reporter may fall into the habit of writing the story in those terms. The officials may be concerned with how the tax rate will affect the municipal budget, so information may come in that form. However, a good reporter will make the effort to figure out how many dollars a typical taxpayer will be paying before and after the change. A story about a change in real estate rates always should include a sentence such as the following: "An owner of a $100,000 home will pay $950 in real estate tax under the new rate, compared with $850 last year."

A routine traffic accident report from the police department may focus on the driver of a car that struck a utility pole. But a reporter thinking of how the accident affected readers may want to focus on the number of households that lost power because of the accident or the number of commuters stuck in the traffic jam caused by the accident.

6. DON'T PRINT ANYTHING YOU DON'T UNDERSTAND. DO NOT TRY TO FAKE YOUR WAY AROUND INFORMATION THAT YOU DON'T UNDERSTAND. GET SOMEONE TO EXPLAIN IT TO YOU, AND THEN EXPLAIN IT TO THE READERS

There is a natural human tendency to want to conceal our ignorance. Sometimes we hate to admit that we don't understand a subject. If you are making small talk at a party, you may be able to just "fake it" without serious consequences. When you are writing a news story, however, the results can be disastrous.

A student journalist once attempted to write a story about a proposal to change the system of awarding tenure to faculty members. The reporter interviewed several people about the subject and got some quotes but never dared to admit that she had no idea what they were talking about. The resulting story described a change in the "ten year plan."

The lesson that this student eventually learned is that it is always better to admit your ignorance and ask someone to explain the subject to you. Most sources find it refreshing to talk to a reporter who is willing to say, "I'm sorry, but I don't know much about this subject at all. Could you please give me a layman's explanation?" In some situations it is possible to get the information by reading books or magazine articles or doing online research. There are many ways to find the information that you are missing, but the most important thing to remember is that you should never attempt to write a story when you don't know what you're writing about.

7. NEVER ASSUME ANYTHING. WHEN IN DOUBT, LEAVE IT OUT. IF YOU MAKE ERRONEOUS ASSUMPTIONS, YOU ARE SPREADING MISINFORMATION

Most of us have been exposed to a teacher who writes the word *ASSUME* on the board and draws two vertical lines to demonstrate that when you assume, "You make an *ASS* of *U* and *ME*." In the world of journalism, when you assume something, you damage the credibility of your newspaper. Good journalists will only report things that they know to be true, assuming nothing.

The worst assumption of all is to assume that nothing important will happen in the last few minutes of a meeting, so it is safe to leave early. The first time you assume this is the time a last-minute challenge will invalidate an earlier decision you reported or a fistfight will break out between two town council members.

If you are on deadline and cannot confirm a piece of information, it is better to leave it out than to include an assumption about which you are not positive. This is why editors fall back on the aphorism, "When in doubt, leave it out."

8. PLAN WHAT YOU CAN, AND BE PREPARED FOR CHANGE. THIS RULE APPLIES TO ALL LEVELS OF JOURNALISM, INCLUDING INTERVIEWS, LEADS, STORY CONSTRUCTION, PAGE LAYOUT, AND EDITION PLANNING

Having a plan is essential. It would be foolhardy to try to conduct an interview, write a story, lay out a page, or produce an edition of a newspaper without having a plan.

Time spent in advance planning almost always pays off in efficiency when the actual production begins.

Of course, the news business is not like a routine assembly process. Fortunately, the unexpected does come up. If it didn't, there would be no news. Good journalists therefore embrace the unexpected and modify their plans to accommodate changing circumstances. If there were no plan to modify, changing circumstances would only add chaos to confusion.

Thus, if you are assigned to write a feature about an outstanding student graduating from the local high school as valedictorian, you will want to prepare a list of questions about the student's academic success and extracurricular activities. If you discover partway through the interview that the student also built a computer from parts and operates a computer-repair business and Web design and hosting network as a sideline, that might alter your plans and suggest a new angle for the story.

9. MAKE EVERY WORD COUNT. DO NOT EXPECT READERS TO WADE THROUGH UNNECESSARY WORDS

In the words of William Strunk, Jr., "Omit needless words." Read over every story to find the extra words. Be particularly suspicious of adjectives and adverbs, which are the weakest parts of speech. Also, look for extra sentences and paragraphs. Double-check the last paragraph; if you placed it last because it is least important, perhaps it should be eliminated altogether.

Can you change "stated that" to "said"? Can you change "in the event that" to "if"? Can you shorten, simplify, or otherwise cut out extra words? If you can, do so.

10. "ACCURACY, ACCURACY, ACCURACY!" JOSEPH PULITZER'S THREE RULES OF JOURNALISM ARE STILL THE PRIME DIRECTIVE

There is no higher praise for a news story than to say that it is accurate, and there is no harsher condemnation than to say that it is inaccurate. When readers see a story with factual errors or errors in spelling, punctuation, or grammar, they lose confidence in the publication.

A tour guide once asked me to write a story about a new guidebook to Cape Cod she had written and self-published. I was working as a travel editor at the Cape Cod Times at the time. I glanced through the book and turned to the neighborhood where I lived, on the north side of Dennis. The book mentioned my favorite ice cream shop, the Ice Cream Smuggler. It said that the shop was housed in one of the oldest buildings on Cape Cod. I found that remarkable, since I had personally witnessed the building being erected in the early 1980s. About two blocks away is the Josiah Dennis Manse, which was built in 1736. I declined to review the book because that one inaccuracy cast doubt on the entire book. If the tour guide got that wrong, how could I trust anything else in the book? Readers of news stories feel the same way. If one fact is wrong, they suspect everything else in the story.

A Stylebook Primer

WHAT IS A STYLEBOOK?

The word *style* has many meanings in the English language. Even within the field of writing, *style* can be used in several ways. Sometimes it is used to mean the individual use of creative techniques by a writer. Sometimes it is used to refer to a genre or type of writing. However, in news writing, *style* refers to the set of usage policies adopted by a publication.

A set of style or usage policies, usually compiled into a *stylebook*, is necessary because there are many options in the English language. For example, in deciding whether to use the numeral *1* or the word *one*, there is no absolutely right or wrong answer. It depends on the policy adopted by the publication. The word *adviser* is sometimes spelled *advisor.* Either can be considered correct, but a publication should be consistent. If decisions such as this were made on a case-by-case basis, editing would become much more complicated and time-consuming.

Reporters and copy editors should be thoroughly familiar with the style policies of their newspapers. Copy editors double-check to make sure that the spelling, punctuation, grammar, and style are in accordance with the newspaper's policies. A more detailed explanation of editing appears in Chapter 32.

Almost all newspapers follow the *Associated Press Stylebook.* The Associated Press (AP) is a cooperative organization of newspapers that agree to share stories and information. The cost of membership in the AP depends on the circulation of the newspaper. Since the AP stories used by hundreds of newspapers are already edited according to AP style, it makes sense for the newspapers to adopt the same style for their locally written stories. Some newspapers, such as *The New York Times,* have their own stylebooks, but they generally have few differences from the AP guidelines.

Anyone interested in pursuing a career in journalism should purchase a copy of the *Associated Press Stylebook* and be familiar with AP style. The *Associated Press Stylebook* is available from the AP and at most bookstores. Updated editions are published periodically.

The following brief list includes a few examples of AP style:

1. ABBREVIATIONS

In general, the stylebook says to avoid an alphabet soup. Do not use abbreviations or acronyms that the reader will not recognize quickly. For example, do not subject readers to sentences such as, "The CEO of ITT told the CFO to OK the RAM upgrade ASAP."

Abbreviate long months (i.e., Jan., Feb., Aug., Sept., Oct., Nov., and Dec.) when part of a date (Sept. 9, 2011). Spell out months otherwise. (He left in September.) Always spell out short months (i.e., March, April, May, June, and July).

Abbreviate states, using the long, old-fashioned abbreviations when used with a town or city, such as Springfield, Mass., Baltimore, Md., Billings, Mont., or Syracuse, N.Y. (If the full mailing address, including ZIP code, is given, then use the Postal Service abbreviation, such as MA, MD, MT, or NY.)

Use periods in the abbreviations for U.S. and U.N., but do not for most others, such as the FBI, CIA, NAACP, AARP, or ABC News. When in doubt, spell them out.

2. CAPITALIZATION

Do not capitalize a word unless you have a good reason to do so. Do capitalize names of people (Mary Jones), proper names (The Smithsonian Institution), companies (Gulf Oil Co.), places (Cape Cod), and months (October).

3. COMPOSITION TITLES

Titles of books, movies, operas, plays, poems, songs, albums, speeches, and works of art all follow the same general pattern. Capitalize the principal words, and enclose the title in quotation marks. Capitalize but do not use quotation marks for the Bible and reference works, such as almanacs and dictionaries.

4. GENERAL USAGE

Write in the third person (i.e., he, she, or it). Avoid the first person (i.e., I or me) and the second person (i.e., you).

Omit unnecessary zeroes. Use 8 p.m. (*not* 8:00 p.m.) and $7 (*not* $7.00).

Use the time-date-place pattern to tell when something is happening. For example, the meeting is 12:30 p.m. Thursday in the Civic Center.

5. NAMES AND TITLES

Identify people by first name and last name on first reference. Identify them by last name only on later references in the same story. Check a person's title or job carefully. In general, use the title *Dr.* only to refer to medical doctors. If it is important to know that a person has a doctorate in history, for example, explain that in the text.

Capitalize titles if they are used before names. Do not capitalize titles after names (e.g., Sheriff Mary Ferguson or Mary Ferguson, sheriff).

Titles of books, articles, songs, television shows, albums, and other compositions should be capitalized and put in quotation marks. Do not underline or use italics.

6. NUMBERS

In general, use words for numbers one through nine, and use figures for numbers 10 and above. Always use figures for addresses, ages, dates, dimensions, distances, heights, page numbers, prices, room numbers, sizes, and years. Use numbers for percentages, and use the word *percent* (not the symbol %).

7. SPELLING

Some of these words may be spelled two ways in English usage but only one way in AP style. Others have only one correct spelling in American English but are frequently misspelled. Make sure that you memorize the following words:

accommodate

adviser

a lot (two words)

all right (two words)

ax

canceled

compatible

consensus

gray

judgment

liaison

occurred

OK, OK'd, OK'ing, OKs

protester

recommended

restaurateur

rock 'n' roll

sheriff

8. THE INTERNET

The AP rules for some Internet terms are different from common usage:

Internet is capitalized, but *intranet* is lowercase.

Offline and *online* are always written as one word.

World Wide Web is capitalized.

Web site is two words with a capital *W*.

Early in my reporting career I discovered the importance of knowing the AP Stylebook. I handed in a story with some style errors. My city editor picked up a copy of the AP Stylebook and tossed it onto my desk. It landed with a loud thump.

"This is yours," he said, "I want you to take it home and put it next to your toilet. Tomorrow, read all the A's. The next day, read all the B's. In 26 days, I expect you to have the whole damn thing memorized. Got it?"

I got it.

How to Read a Newspaper

1. IT IS IMPORTANT FOR A JOURNALIST TO READ A NEWSPAPER EVERY DAY

Anyone who aspires to write news must read news. A daily dose of news gets you used to the rhythm of how news stories are written. Although it is possible to keep abreast of current events through radio, television, or the Internet, it is much easier to analyze the writing involved by reading a newspaper. Although there has been a decline in newspaper circulation in recent years, that is still where the best news writing is found.

The entire content of a half-hour news broadcast could be transcribed on less than one page of a newspaper. This indicates how much more information is available in printed form. Furthermore, a person can read a news story much more quickly than a broadcast reporter can present it aloud.

2. A JOURNALIST SHOULD READ A VARIETY OF NEWSPAPERS AND CHECK OUT OTHER SOURCES OF NEWS

It helps to read different newspapers to see how various writers and editors handled the same stories. It also helps to compare coverage among newspapers, newsmagazines, radio, television, and various Internet reports. A good writer will follow the best examples, not the most common.

3. NEWSPAPERS ARE DESIGNED FOR SCANNING; YOU DO NOT HAVE TO READ EVERY WORD OF EVERY STORY

It would be impractical to read every word of a newspaper. Most papers include a variety of stories to appeal to a variety of people. Some people may want to read all the sports coverage and skip the business news; others may take the opposite approach. Most people will read the beginning of a story to decide whether they want to continue.

4. LOOK FOR THE ORGANIZATIONAL STRUCTURE OF THE NEWSPAPER YOU ARE READING AND USE IT TO YOUR ADVANTAGE

Most editors work hard to organize their newspapers into sections and departments. Good papers cluster related stories together. It may help to flip through the whole paper to see how it is organized so that you can turn to your favorite areas easily. Check for an index or table of contents to help you find your way around the paper.

5. MAKE SURE YOU DISTINGUISH BETWEEN NEWS AND ADVERTISING

Good newspapers maintain a virtual brick wall between news and advertising. A discriminating reader should be aware of the difference.

Usually, advertising is located on the bottom parts of pages and is enclosed in a box or border of some kind. Advertising should be printed in a different typeface from news. The person who pays for the ad determines the content of the advertising. On the other hand, the editor determines the content of news stories and editorials. Advertising is usually one-sided and designed to entice the reader to purchase a product or service. News and editorial matter should be more balanced. It may be more difficult—but equally important—to distinguish between news and advertising in the emerging new digital media.

6. WITHIN THE EDITORIAL DEPARTMENT, DISTINGUISH BETWEEN OPINION PIECES AND NEWS

After distinguishing between advertising and news, there is still another distinction to be made. Good editors include both news and opinion in their newspapers, and the distinction should be clear and obvious to the readers. Usually, there are one or two specially designated opinion pages. On an opinion page, you will find an editorial, which is the editorial opinion of the newspaper, typically unsigned. It is supposed to represent the collective opinion of the newspaper's editorial board. Also on an opinion page you typically will find opinion columns in which commentators express informed opinions on vital interests of the day. Good newspapers print letters to the editor, in which ordinary readers express their opinions. Another popular feature of opinion pages is the editorial cartoon. None of these is expected to be objective and unbiased.

News stories, on the other hand, are supposed to be objective, balanced, and fair, allowing readers to make up their own minds. Unless it is made clear that what you are reading is supposed to be an opinion, you should expect the writing to be as objective as possible under the circumstances.

7. AMONG THE NEWS STORIES, DISTINGUISH BETWEEN STRAIGHT, OR HARD, NEWS STORIES AND OTHER TYPES OF NEWS WRITING, INCLUDING FEATURE STORIES, REVIEWS, ADVICE COLUMNS, GUIDES AND LISTINGS, AND SPECIAL FEATURES

Even after setting aside all the advertising and all the opinion-page material, newspapers still present a variety of material. A basic news story, often called *straight news* or *hard news,* will be very straightforward, giving only the facts of a news event. However, there are also feature stories, which may use special writing techniques to enhance interest in a story that is of interest for reasons other than its timeliness or significance. Other special features found in newspapers include such things as entertainment reviews and previews, advice columns, and special features such as humor columns, comics, and horoscopes that are included to entertain or amuse the reader.

8. NOTICE THE DESIGN OF THE NEWSPAPER. IS IT WELL ORGANIZED?

Newspaper design has evolved over the last 350 years. Most newspapers began the twenty-first century using modular design, which arranges elements in regular rectangles that are easy to read. Large photographs, often in color, enhance these papers. A good designer includes enough white space to separate different items on a page, creating a pleasing effect. If the paper is well designed, you will find it easy to read and easy to find the areas that interest you.

9. LOOK FOR CORRECTIONS. IF A NEWSPAPER ACKNOWLEDGES ITS MISTAKES AND CORRECTS THEM IN A TIMELY FASHION, THIS IS A SIGN THAT IT IS A QUALITY PUBLICATION

It is impossible to publish a newspaper without making mistakes. Good newspapers acknowledge this and publish corrections when warranted. Most designate a certain place or a certain page for corrections. If a newspaper never publishes a correction, this does not mean that it has never made an error; it merely means that it refuses to admit its errors.

10. LOOK FOR LETTERS TO THE EDITOR. IF A NEWSPAPER PRESENTS A VARIETY OF OPINIONS, THIS IS ALSO A GOOD SIGN

A lively collection of letters to the editor shows that the readers are engaged with the newspaper and consider it a worthy means of communication. It is a particularly healthy sign if a newspaper includes letters that criticize its own policies or decisions.

11. STARTING WITH PAGE ONE IS USUALLY A GOOD IDEA

With such a variety of information, where does a reader start? Page one is where the editor places the most important and most interesting stories of the edition. Therefore, a reader would do well to begin by looking briefly at each of the stories on the front page. They represent the editor's top recommendations. Sometimes a story that might not seem newsworthy at first is placed on page one because of some other merit. It might be particularly well written, ironic, or touching.

12. BRIEFLY SCAN THE ENTIRE NEWSPAPER, GLANCING AT THE HEADLINES, TO SEE IF THERE IS SOMETHING UNEXPECTEDLY INTERESTING

After looking over the front page, look through the paper, glancing at photographs, headlines, and anything that catches your eye. You may want to stop and read a story right away, or you may want to make a mental note to return to something later.

13. CHECK OUT YOUR FAVORITE SECTIONS OR PAGES, AND LOOK FOR YOUR FAVORITE WRITERS

Sports fans may want to go straight to the sports section. Investors may want to check out the stock market listings. Political junkies may want to read their favorite political columnists. Maybe the weather forecast or comics pages interest you most. Surveys show that many readers turn to the advice columns or obituaries first.

14. IF A HEADLINE INDICATES THAT A STORY IS ABOUT SOMETHING OF NO INTEREST TO YOU, DON'T WASTE YOUR TIME ON IT

Readers are under no obligation to read stories they don't care about. If you see a headline that tells you that the tax rate is changing in a community where you don't know anybody, maybe you don't care. Unlike TV viewer a newspaper reader instantly can move on to the next story.

15. IF A HEADLINE INDICATES THAT YOU MAY HAVE SOME INTEREST, READ THE FIRST FEW PARAGRAPHS

Perhaps the headline does catch your attention. The headline summarizes the story in six or eight words. The reader's next step is to read the first few paragraphs. This is called the *lead*. The lead summarizes the story in 30 to 100 words. By that point you should have a good idea what the story is all about. If you don't, the story is probably poorly written.

16. AS YOU READ A NEWS STORY, LOOK TO SEE IF THE REPORTER ANSWERS ALL THE BASIC QUESTIONS AND INCLUDES ALL THE IMPORTANT POINTS OF VIEW

Does the reporter tell you who, what, where, when, why, and how? Do you learn the location, time, and impact of the event quickly? In a well-written story, you will. If the story involves a controversy, does the reporter present both points of view? A good reporter will.

17. IF THE STORY IS ABOUT A SUBJECT THAT REALLY INTERESTS YOU, READ IT ALL THE WAY TO THE END

If it is a well-written story about an interesting subject, sit back and relax. You may want to fold the newspaper to a size that is easy to handle. Read the whole story. There may be surprising tidbits scattered throughout the story. Chances are that the version in the newspaper will be more comprehensive than the shorter version presented on television news. There may be references to other sources of information, such as Web sites or related articles. Notice what you liked about the story. You might be able to use some of the same techniques yourself.

Commonly Misused Words

Journalists must be experts in the correct use of language. Just as a mistake in accuracy will undermine the credibility of a story, a mistake in grammar, diction, or usage can make a reader suspect everything else in the article.

Reporters who make elementary mistakes, such as confusing *it's* with *its,* will lose the respect of their readers and probably lose their jobs. Anyone who has trouble with these words should make a concerted study of them to correct that problem.

Here are sets of words that writers commonly confuse:

1. IT'S/ITS

It's is a contraction for *it is.* It should be used sparingly. In formal writing, it is generally better to spell out *it is. Its* means "belonging to it." It is a possessive pronoun, like *his, hers, theirs, ours,* and *yours,* none of which has an apostrophe.

2. THERE/THEY'RE/THEIR

There is an adverb meaning "in or at that place." Note the similarity between *here* and *there. They're* is a contraction for *they are.* It should be used sparingly. In formal writing, it is generally better to spell out *they are. Their* is an adjective meaning "of or relating to them."

3. AFFECT/EFFECT

The words *affect* and *effect* both have primary and secondary uses, a complication that confuses many people. In most situations, it is best to learn the primary uses and avoid the secondary uses.

The Primary Uses

Affect is usually a verb meaning "to influence or produce a change."

> The weather affects people's mood.
> Pollution affects fish.

> Remember: To *affect* is to take action.

> *Effect* is usually a noun meaning "a result."

> The music had an effect on the audience.
> The pollution had an effect on the fish.

> Remember: An *effect* is an end result.

The Secondary Uses

Affect also can be used as a noun meaning "a feeling or emotion," but this is best avoided. *Effect* also can be used as a verb meaning "to produce or bring about," usually in a phrase such as *to effect a change*, but this is also best avoided.

These secondary uses of *affect* and *effect* are found most frequently in academic writing. They are acceptable in doctoral dissertations, but they only add to confusion when used in newspapers.

4. THEN/THAN

Then is an adverb meaning "at that time" or "next in time or order." Remember: Then refers to elapsed time or sequence. *Than* is a comparative conjunction used to express preference or difference. Remember: Than makes a comparison.

Consider the following sentences:

I would rather kiss you than make love.
I would rather kiss you *then* make love.

It is important to understand the difference.

After these "big four," there are plenty of other troublesome homonyms—words that sound the same but have different meanings and spellings. Here are a few to watch:

5. BY/BUY/BYE

By is a preposition meaning "beside" or "near." *Buy* is a verb meaning "to purchase." *Bye* is a shortened form of *good-bye*, a noun or interjection used as a statement of farewell. In sports, *bye* is a position of a player who does not face opposition in the early rounds of a tournament.

I went to the drug store by the town hall to buy a card to say bye to my friend, who was leaving town.

6. CITE/SIGHT/SITE

Cite is a verb meaning "to refer to." *Sight* is a noun meaning "the ability to see" or "something seen." *Site* is a noun meaning "a location."

In the future, historians will cite the dramatic photograph that captured the sight of the flag being raised over the site of the World Trade Center.

7. COUNCIL/COUNSEL

Council is a noun meaning "a group empowered to make decisions." *Counsel* is a noun meaning "an adviser" or a verb meaning "to advise."

The town council hired a legal counsel to provide the group with legal advice.

8. TO/TOO/TWO

To is a preposition meaning "in the direction of." *Too* is an adverb meaning "excessively." (*The word has too many O's.*) *Two* is a numerical adjective meaning "one more than one in number."

The two girls went to the mall where they bought too much stuff.

9. WHO'S/WHOSE

Who's is a contraction for *who is*. *Whose* is a possessive adjective or pronoun meaning "belonging to whom." (Remember, possessive pronouns do not have apostrophes.)

Who's going to decide whose responsibility it is to clean up this mess?

Although not homonyms, here are a couple more troublesome pairs of words:

10. FARTHER/FURTHER

Farther is an adverb meaning "at a greater distance." *Further* is an adverb meaning "to a greater extent." Although these words sometimes are used interchangeably in general English usage, in news writing it is best to use *farther* for distance and *further* for degree.

As she went further in her education, she had to attend schools farther from her home.

11. LAY/LIE AND SET/SIT

Lay is a transitive verb meaning "to place or put" (something). Its past tense is *laid*.

Usually I lay the book on the table.
Last night I laid the book on the floor.

Lie is an intransitive verb that means "to recline." The past tense is *lay* (which adds to the confusion between these two words).

Usually I lie down after dinner
Last night I lay down before dinner.

Lie is also an intransitive verb meaning "to utter a falsehood." The past tense of that word is *lied*.

It is not ethical to lie.
The reporter was fired because he lied.

Set is a transitive verb meaning "to place or put" (something). Its past tense is *set*.

Usually I set the book on the table.
Last night I set the book on the floor.

(Note that *set* is nearly a synonym to *lay*, although in common usage the words are employed in different situations.) *Sit* is an intransitive verb meaning "to assume a seated position." The past tense is *sat*.

Usually I sit down for dinner.
Last night I sat down for dinner.

And here are two important notes about phrases that are not words:

12. ALL RIGHT/A LOT

Alright is not a word in standard usage. The correct phrase is *all right*.

In newspapers, it is not all right to use the nonstandard slang term "alright."

Alot is not a word in standard usage. The correct phrase is *a lot*.

The misspelling of the phrase "a lot" as one word is not correct, despite the fact that you see it a lot in Internet chat rooms.

Punctuation

This chapter highlights the most common use of punctuation. For further guidance, consult any standard grammar book. The most commonly used—and misused—punctuation mark is the comma. Contrary to popular belief commas do not signal a "natural pause" in a sentence. Almost all proper uses of a comma will be covered by one of the eight rules given here.

1. COMMAS SEPARATE ITEMS IN A SERIES

Newspaper ink comes in magenta, cyan, yellow and black.
The sad, tired, old farmer was difficult to interview.

In news writing, reporters do not use a comma before the conjunction that precedes the final item. The Associated Press Stylebook says: "Use commas to separate elements in a series, but do not put a comma before the conjunction in a simple series: "The flag is red, white and blue."

The stylebook does go on to advise that there are times when that final comma is needed for clarity, such as when the items in the series contain a conjunction themselves or are long and complicated.

(Other types of writing do use a comma before the conjunction, even in a simple series. For example, *The Elements of Style,* by Strunk and White, says: "In a series of three or more terms with a single conjunction, use a comma after each term except the last." "Thus write, 'red, white, and blue.'" This style is used in this textbook. Nevertheless, newspaper editors will expect reporters to know that the *Associated Press Stylebook* makes an exception to Strunk and White in this case.)

2. COMMAS SET OFF PARENTHETICAL INFORMATION THAT COULD BE REMOVED FROM THE SENTENCE WITHOUT CHANGING ITS MEANING

Mary Smith, who missed five classes, failed the course.

Commas should not set off restrictive or essential words, phrases, and clauses.

Students who miss too many classes fail their courses.

When it comes to this use of the comma, grammar books tend to devote lots of space to what grammarians call "nonessential" or "nonrestrictive" phrases and clauses, all of which can be considered parenthetical information. However, a simple way to remember them is that they could be removed from the sentence without altering the basic meaning. In the first example above, Mary Smith failed the course. No matter what is inserted between the commas, she still flunked. The material between the commas could, in fact, be placed between parentheses, which is why it is called parenthetical information. It must be set off by commas.

Contrast this with the second example above, which says that students who miss too many classes fail their classes. In that example, the phrase "who miss too many classes" is essential to the meaning of the sentence. If it were removed, the sentence "Students fail their classes" means something different. Such restrictive or essential phrases should not be set off by commas.

3. COMMAS ARE USED BEFORE A COORDINATING CONJUNCTION THAT JOINS TWO INDEPENDENT CLAUSES

The reporter was getting stonewalled, but she doggedly pursued the information.

The comma may be omitted if the clause is very short.

The reporter was getting stonewalled and she quit.

The main thing to remember with this rule is that commas are used before a coordinating conjunction that joins two independent clauses.

What is a coordinating conjunction? It is a conjunction that can join two independent clauses. Some people just recognize them when they see them; others like to memorize them. If you like memory devices, remember *fanboys,* which stands for the seven coordinating conjunctions: *for, and, not, but, or, yet,* and *so.*

What is an independent clause? It is a group of words that could be written as a complete sentence but is, instead, combined with another phrase or clause. If it is combined with another independent clause, your best bet is to join them with a comma and a coordinating conjunction. For example, "I like cake" could be a complete sentence. "I like ice cream" could be a complete sentence. If you want to combine them as two independent clauses, though, combine them with a comma and a coordinating conjunction: "I like cake, and I like ice cream."

When considering this rule, you also should consider other options for combining two independent clauses. One option is to use a conjunctive adverb (such as *however, hence,* or *therefore*) that is preceded by a semicolon and followed by a comma. Another option is to use a semicolon alone between the two clauses. A third option is to make them two separate sentences with a period between them. If there is a conjunctive adverb or if there is no conjunction between the independent clauses, a semicolon or period is needed.

These are all valid options:

I like cake; however, I like ice cream more.

I like cake; I like ice cream.

I like cake. I like ice cream.

She was getting stonewalled; however, she doggedly pursued the information.

The reporter was getting stonewalled; she quit.

4. COMMAS USUALLY SEPARATE DIRECT QUOTATIONS FROM THE ATTRIBUTION

Commas are used to introduce a complete, one-sentence quotation.

The Elements of Style *says, "Omit needless words."*

Commas are used before a closing quotation mark that is followed by attribution.

"Always put commas inside quotation marks," the textbook says.

Commas are not used when a quotation that is not a complete sentence follows the attribution.

The book says to follow this rule "without exception."

In news writing, the most common form of attribution is the phrase "he said" or "she said" immediately after a complete sentence. Such a sentence, which ordinarily would end with a period, should end with a comma and the closing quotation mark, followed by the attribution and the period.

"I never had sexual relations with that woman," he said.
"Taxes are for little people," she said.

5. COMMAS SET OFF WORDS OF DIRECT ADDRESS FROM THE REST OF A SENTENCE

Put down that chain saw, Grandma, before you hurt someone.
"Frankly, my dear, I don't give a damn," said Rhett Butler.

Direct address is used rarely in news writing unless it appears in a quotation. This rule is closely related to the second rule because the words of direct address could be removed without changing the meaning of the sentence.

The second example above, from the classic film *Gone With the Wind,* created quite a stir when the film was released in 1939 because it was shocking to hear the word *damn* in a feature film. The example demonstrates both rules 4 and 5.

6. IN NUMBERS, COMMAS SEPARATE THOUSANDS FROM HUNDREDS AND MILLIONS FROM HUNDRED THOUSANDS

The car I want costs $35,000. The house I want costs $1,750,000.

Most people learned this rule in third or fourth grade. In America, we count left from the decimal point and insert a comma after every three digits. The Associated Press Stylebook says to do this for all numbers over 999, except for street addresses, broadcast frequencies, room numbers, serial numbers, telephone numbers, and years.

7. COMMAS ARE USED TO SEPARATE INTRODUCTORY WORDS, PHRASES, AND CLAUSES FROM THE MAIN CLAUSE OF THE SENTENCE

Under the circumstances, I think you should leave town.

The first step in using this rule is to identify a main clause, which is a group of words that could stand alone as a separate sentence. If such a clause exists and there is an introductory group of words before it, then separate them with a comma.

Because I work so hard, I go to bed early.

The comma is optional if the introduction is just one or two words.

Usually I go to bed early.

8. COMMAS ARE USED TO SET OFF YEARS IN DATES AND CITIES AND STATES IN ADDRESSES

On April 1, 1981, I moved to 39 Walnut Bottom Road, Laurel, Md., for a year.
I lived in Norfolk, Va., and Palo Alto, Calif., before moving to Dennis, Mass.

These are referred to in most grammar books as "conventional uses" of the comma because they do not reflect the structural grammar of the sentence so much as the stylistic conventions that Americans have adopted for writing dates and place names.

Remember when writing dates that the year is set off by commas both before and after. Similarly, when writing a city and state, the state is set off by commas both before and after. If the complete address is given, the city is also set off with commas both before and after.

If a state name is used and it does not follow the name of a town or city, the state name should be spelled out, not abbreviated.

When the state name follows a city, most newspapers follow AP style, which calls for using the traditional abbreviations, such as *Md., Mass., Mich., Minn., Miss., Mo., Mont.,* etc., in the text of news stories. Short state names, such as *Maine,* are not abbreviated. If the full mailing address including ZIP code is given, then use the Postal Service abbreviation, such as *MD, MA, ME, MI, MN, MS, MO, MT,* etc. The United States Postal Service abbreviations are used in situations where a reader may want to copy the complete address for addressing an envelope. They do not take periods.

9. USE A SEMICOLON TO SEPARATE TWO CLOSELY RELATED INDEPENDENT CLAUSES

I don't want to go home; I want to stay right here.

A writer must decide whether to make two clauses separate sentences or combine them into one. If they are to be combined, the writer must decide whether to use a conjunction and a comma or simply to use a semicolon. The following example indicates a close relation between the clauses:

She was born in Hawaii; she learned to surf before she was 4.

The next example, however, does not have such a close relationship, so the conjunction and comma technique seems to make more sense:

She was born in Hawaii, but she moved to Alaska when she was 4.

10. USE SEMICOLONS TO SEPARATE TWO INDEPENDENT CLAUSES THAT ARE JOINED BY A CONJUNCTIVE ADVERB

I don't want to go home; however, I don't want to stay here either.

Conjunctive adverbs such as *however* and *therefore* do more than link two clauses, like conjunctions. They also tell the reader something about the relationship, like adverbs. Many of them can be used as simple adverbs that just modify a verb, but when they connect two independent clauses, they take on the role of conjunctive adverbs. They include also, *finally, furthermore, however, incidentally, likewise, meanwhile, moreover, namely, nevertheless, otherwise, similarly,* and *therefore.*

If you find yourself in such a situation, be sure to use a semicolon before the conjunctive adverb and a comma after it; however, it might be simpler to rewrite the sentence as two separate sentences.

11. USE A SEMICOLON TO SEPARATE ITEMS IN A SERIES WHEN THE ITEMS CONTAIN COMMAS

I have lived in Boston, Mass.; Baltimore, Md.; Cleveland, Ohio; and Athens, Ga.

We all know to use commas to separate items in a series, but sometimes we have to move up to the semicolon level because the items in the series have their own commas. If we used commas to separate the items in the series, the reader would not be able to tell where one item of the series ends and the next one begins. This comes up often with lists of people and their hometowns, as in a list of survivors in an obituary or a list of candidates and their offices.

He is survived by a sister, Susan Foster of Marietta, Ga.; a son, John Smith of Silver Spring, Md.; a daughter, Mary Smith of Missoula, Mont.; and several nieces and nephews.

Student government leaders elected include Linda Goldberg, president; David Chung, vice president; and Luis Martinez, secretary.

Note that the semicolon is used before the final conjunction, even though a comma would not be used in the equivalent situation when following AP style.

12. USE A COLON AFTER AN INDEPENDENT CLAUSE TO INTRODUCE A LIST

Students should come to class with three things: a textbook, a notebook and a pen.

The same rule applies whether the items in the list appear as part of a normal paragraph or they are broken out as a bulleted or numbered list.

There are eight states that are never abbreviated in the text of news stories:

- Alaska
- Hawaii
- Idaho
- Iowa
- Maine
- Ohio
- Texas
- Utah

Note that you should only use a colon before a list if the words before the colon constitute an independent clause, which means that they could stand alone as a complete sentence. Do not use a colon if the list is part of the main clause.

Students should come to class with a textbook, a notebook and a pen.

13. USE A COLON BEFORE A LONG QUOTATION OF MORE THAN ONE SENTENCE

John Lennon wrote: "You may say that I'm a dreamer. But I'm not the only one. I hope someday you'll join us, and the world will live as one."

Usually a comma is used between attribution and a following quote, but when the quotation is longer than usual, a colon may be used. When the attribution is in one paragraph and the quotation follows as a separate paragraph, a colon must be used at the end of the attribution.

Officer Thomas O'Malley described the incident this way:
"It all started when the first driver slammed on the brakes to avoid a duck that was crossing the road. Then a second car hit the rear of the first car . . ."

14. HYPHENS ARE CONNECTORS; DASHES ARE SEPARATORS

Hyphens are short lines that connect two words. Dashes are long lines that separate words. A well-used hyphen helps readers—who may or may not understand grammar—find their way through a sentence. (The preceding sentence demonstrates the use of one hyphen and a pair of dashes.)

15. APOSTROPHES ARE USED TO INDICATE POSSESSION IN NOUNS AND TO INDICATE OMITTED LETTERS IN CONTRACTIONS

Although apostrophes show possession in nouns (such as *John's pen*), and in contractions (such as *it's* for *it is*), they are never used in possessive pronouns (such as *yours, mine, his hers,* or *its*).

Punctuating Quotations

1. THE COMMA OR PERIOD AT THE END OF A QUOTATION ALWAYS SHOULD BE PLACED INSIDE THE QUOTATION MARKS

Wrong: Isak Dinesen said, "I write a little every day without hope and without despair".
Right: Isak Dinesen said, "I write a little every day without hope and without despair."

This rule has more to do with typography than logic. Printers decided long ago that the little punctuation mark (period or comma) hanging outside the closing quotation looked bad, so the convention in America has been to keep it inside. This dates back at least to William Strunk's first edition of *The Elements of Style*, written in 1918, in which he says, "Typographical usage dictates that the comma be inside the marks, though logically it often seems not to belong there."

Incidentally, the rule is not followed in Great Britain. In American news writing or any standard American writing, however, always put the period or comma before the closing quotation mark.

He says his favorite words are, "compassion," "onomatopoeia," "serendipity" and "effervescence."
"Never look back," said Satchel Paige. "Someone may be gaining on you."

This rule does not apply to other punctuation marks, such as question marks, exclamation points, semicolons, colons, and dashes. For those marks, the placement depends on whether the punctuation applies to the material inside the quotation or to the sentence as a whole.

He referred to the book "Who Moved My Cheese?"
Have you read the book "The Shipping News?"

(Note that titles of books are put in quotation marks in newspapers, whereas they normally would be placed in italics in books or academic compositions.)

2. CAPITALIZE THE FIRST WORD IN A QUOTATION THAT IS A COMPLETE SENTENCE, BUT DO NOT CAPITALIZE THE FIRST WORD IN A QUOTATION THAT IS NOT A COMPLETE SENTENCE

Wrong: He said, "people should look both ways before they cross the street."
Right: He said, "People should look both ways before they cross the street."

This rule applies whether the punctuation preceding the quotation is a comma or a colon. It holds true even if the speaker had uttered other words before or after those quoted. If the words could stand alone as a sentence, then capitalize the first word of the quotation.

3. IF WORDS OF ATTRIBUTION PRECEDE A LONG QUOTATION OF MORE THAN ONE SENTENCE, USE A COLON; OTHERWISE, USE A COMMA

Wrong: Mark Twain said, "I apologize for writing a long letter. If I'd had more time, I'd have written a shorter one."
Right: Mark Twain said: "I apologize for writing a long letter. If I'd had more time, I'd have written a shorter one."

4. THE SIMPLEST FORM OF ATTRIBUTION ("JONES SAID") IS CONSIDERED THE BEST. JOURNALISTS SHOULD AVOID ATTRIBUTIONS THAT TRY TO DO MORE THAN SIMPLY ATTRIBUTE THE QUOTE, SUCH AS "HE CLAIMED," OR "SHE LAUGHED."

Wrong: "I am not a crook," claimed the president.
Right: "I am not a crook," the president said.

For attribution in news writing, stick with said. Whether or not the president is a crook is up to the public to decide, and a journalist can only tell them what the president said. Use of the verb claimed inserts an implication that the statement may be contrary to the truth. Similarly, a word such as confirmed inserts an implication that the statement is accurate. The word said has no such baggage.

Amateur writers and some misguided high school English teachers believe that a writer must avoid repeating words. This sends the poor writer to a thesaurus, which produces a multitude of words that mean nearly the same thing. As Mark Twain said, though, "The difference between the right word and the nearly right word is the same as that between lightning and lightning bug."

The convenient Microsoft Word thesaurus supplies the following words in place of said: *supposed, thought, whispered, alleged, held, believed, understood,* and *assumed.* None of these should appear as attribution in news writing, with the possible exception of *whispered,* if, indeed, the person was whispering. Nor should a news writer fall for *asserted, avowed, chuckled, snorted, laughed, exclaimed, declared, opined, postulated,* or *concluded.*

One reason that *said* works so well is that readers tend to read right over it quickly without noticing it. It communicates the idea that a person is speaking, but it does not get in the way. A news story can use the phrase "she said" repeatedly, and the readers will not be aware of the repetition.

5. IN MOST CASES, THE ATTRIBUTION SHOULD HAVE THE SUBJECT BEFORE THE VERB

Wrong: Said James Thurber: "I consider that that 'that' that worries us so much should be forgotten. Rats desert a sinking ship. That's infest a sinking magazine."
Right: James Thurber said: "I consider that that 'that' that worries us so much should be forgotten. Rats desert a sinking ship. That's infest a sinking magazine."

In news writing, the simpler form is preferred. It is usually preferable to follow the subject-verb-object pattern, which places the name of the speaker before the verb of attribution, usually said. Unless there is a compelling reason to reverse this, stick to "Jones said" rather than "said Jones."

There is no need to worry about inserting variety into the sentence pattern. Readers are reassured—not bored—by consistent patterns.

6. IN NEWS WRITING, UNLESS YOU ARE QUOTING SOMEONE, DO NOT USE QUOTATION MARKS

Wrong: The college is starting a "wicked awesome" new program.
Right: The college is starting a new program.

Of course, the "wrong" example above would be correct if the phrase were attributed to a person who actually did utter the words "wicked awesome." However, it is incorrect to put the words in quotation marks to indicate that it is a trendy new expression.

Unfortunately, the world of advertising is doing a disservice to the English language in this area. Some advertising copywriters use quotation marks as a way to emphasize a word or phrase. In good writing—including good advertising copywriting—the best way to emphasize a word or phrase is through skillful use of the language. Sentence structure, rhythm, word placement, and word choice can direct the readers' attention to a particular word or phrase.

In news writing, quotation marks have a very specific use. They must enclose words that are exactly what a person said. A reporter should never alter a person's words to make the quote sound better. That is unethical. If there is a better way to express what the source said, you can always use an indirect quote, which does not use quotation marks. If you use quotation marks, the words between them must be exactly what the person said.

7. WHEN POSSIBLE MAKE THE START OF A QUOTATION THE START OF A PARAGRAPH

Wrong: Mitchell predicted a dramatic increase in gasoline prices. "It's going to cost twice as much to fill up your tank in a few years," he said.
Right: "It's going to cost twice as much to fill up your tank in a few years," said Mitchell, predicting a dramatic increase in gasoline prices.

Quotations in a news story are like dialogue in a novel. Starting a new paragraph for each speaker makes it easier for the reader. If you have a good quote, highlight it by making it the beginning of the paragraph. Putting explanations in front of a quotation is sometimes called "stepping on the quote."

Active and Passive Voice

1. THE ACTIVE VOICE IS MORE EFFECTIVE THAN THE PASSIVE VOICE IN ALMOST ALL SITUATIONS

Active: The boy hits the ball.
Passive: The ball is hit by the boy.

Both sentences above are correct grammatically, but most writers and readers prefer the one written in active voice. *Voice* is a word that is used many ways in the English language. Even in the field of writing, it can mean different things. Grammatically, however, it refers to a choice in the way we construct sentences. The simpler, more direct way is known as active voice. Use it.

The choice of active or passive voice only applies to sentences with transitive verbs—those that take a direct object. (With intransitive verbs, there is no direct object.)

Note that passive voice is not the same as past tense. Passive-voice sentences can be written in any tense, and past-tense sentences can be either active or passive voice. In *The Elements of Style,* William Strunk, Jr., says, "The active voice is usually more direct and vigorous than the passive."

In the examples above, it is obvious that it is more direct to say, "The boy hit the ball," but some writers fall into the bad habit of using passive-voice constructions without even noticing it. A good writer—especially a news writer—is aware of the differences between active and passive voice and usually selects the active voice.

2. IN AN ACTIVE-VOICE SENTENCE, THE SUBJECT PERFORMS THE ACTION OF THE VERB; IN A PASSIVE-VOICE SENTENCE, THE SUBJECT RECEIVES THE ACTION OF THE VERB

Active: The knight will slay the dragon.
Passive: The dragon will be slain by the knight.

Both active- and passive-voice sentences typically begin with a subject, but in the passive-voice construction, the subject is a receiver of the action of the verb. In the example above, the dragon receives the sword of the knight. In active-voice sentences, the subject does something to the object. In passive-voice sentences, the subject has something done to it.

Active: The center fielder caught the fly ball.
Passive: The fly ball was caught by the center fielder.

3. PASSIVE-VOICE SENTENCES OFTEN USE THE WORD BY TO INDICATE WHO OR WHAT PERFORMED AN ACTION. IN OTHER CASES, THE PERFORMER OF THE ACTION IS OMITTED

Active: The judge sentenced Jones to five years in prison.
Passive: Jones was sentenced to five years in prison.

One of the special characteristics of passive-voice sentences is that the writer can easily omit the person or thing causing the action. In the passive-voice example above, it may be unnecessary to identify the person who imposed the sentence on Jones, but there are other times when the passive voice is used to avoid identifying the main character in a sentence.

Samuel Johnson wrote that "Patriotism is the last refuge of scoundrels." One might say that the passive voice is the last refuge of scoundrels. "Mistakes were made" is a classic passive-voice sentence used to avoid accepting blame. To turn it into an active-voice sentence, we would need to add a subject, such as "I made mistakes."

The same scoundrel who says "Mistakes were made" may reassure us that "Corrective action will be taken." Once again, though, the agent of change is left unstated. If you ever find yourself writing in the passive voice, check to see whether you are concealing the agent of change and decide whether that is a good idea.

4. WRITERS FORM THE PASSIVE VOICE OF A VERB BY COMBINING THE HELPING VERB TO BE WITH THE PAST PARTICIPLE OF THE MAIN VERB

Most word-processing software includes a grammar checker that attempts to identify passive-voice sentences. Because a computer cannot understand the logic or meaning of the sentence, programmers needed to find a more objective way to identify passive-voice sentences. Thus, if the sentence includes any form of the verb *to be* followed by any past participle, the grammar checker will identify that sentence as one that "may be in the passive voice." Good writers, of course, are better than computers at judging the structure of a sentence, and they will double-check the warning.

The forms of the verb *to be* include *is, was, will be, has been, had been,* and *will have been.* The past participles of verbs usually (but not always) end in *-ed.* They are usually (but not always) the same as the past-tense form of the verb. English has enough irregular verbs to keep the best writers on their toes.

These are all passive-voice constructions:

Present: It is eaten. They are seen. I am admired.

Past: It was eaten. They were seen. I was admired.

Future: It will be eaten. They will be seen. I will be admired.

Present perfect: It has been eaten. They have been seen. I have been admired.

Past perfect: It had been eaten. They had been seen. I had been admired.

Future perfect: It will have been eaten. They will have been seen. I will have been admired.

5. TO CHANGE A PASSIVE-VOICE SENTENCE TO ACTIVE VOICE, MAKE THE THING THAT RECEIVES THE ACTION THE OBJECT AT THE END OF THE SENTENCE, AND MAKE THE THING THAT PERFORMS THE ACTION THE SUBJECT AT THE BEGINNING OF THE SENTENCE

Passive: The professor was impressed by the student.
Active: The student impressed the professor.

This is a passive-voice repair kit. Whenever a sentence has a transitive verb, there should be a subject and an object. One of them will be a noun or noun phrase that is the agent of change, the instigator, or the actor. The other will be the receiver of change, the recipient, or the thing acted on. To make the sentence active voice, just make sure that the actor is the subject and that the thing acted on is the object.

In the examples above, the student is the actor. Something the student did created a change in the mind of the professor. Therefore, to change the passive-voice sentence to active voice, just move that student up to the front of the sentence and put the professor at the end.

As indicated earlier, some passive-voice sentences obscure the person or thing responsible for the action. If the instigator of the action is unknown, some words, such as an indefinite noun, may have to be added to create a subject.

Passive: The gravestones were vandalized.
Active: Someone vandalized the gravestones.
Or: Vandals damaged the gravestones.

6. USE THE ACTIVE VOICE FOR FORCEFUL, DIRECT WRITING THAT EMPHASIZES THE PERSON OR THING DOING THE ACTING

Active: John F. Kennedy captured the imagination of young Americans.
Passive: The imagination of young Americans was captured by John F. Kennedy.

Like President Kennedy, active-voice writing is noted for its vigor. It is usually more direct and sounds more sincere.

Active: I love you.
Passive: You are loved by me.

7. USE THE PASSIVE VOICE IN CERTAIN TYPES OF SCIENTIFIC WRITING IN WHICH THE ACTION TAKEN IS MORE IMPORTANT, AND THE PERSON TAKING THE ACTION IS IRRELEVANT

Active: Those conducting the experiment added five milligrams of sodium chloride to each sample.
Passive: Five milligrams of sodium chloride was added to each sample.

This is one of the few times where passive voice is preferable. The convention in some types of scientific writing, such as laboratory reports, is to avoid any reference to the people conducting the experiment.

8. USE THE PASSIVE VOICE WHEN THE RECIPIENT OF THE ACTION IS MORE IMPORTANT THAN THE ACTOR

Active: An assassin shot and killed President John Fitzgerald Kennedy today.
Passive: President John Fitzgerald Kennedy was shot and killed by an assassin today.

This passive-voice sentence is the lead of Tom Wicker's story in the late edition of *The New York Times* on Nov. 22, 1963. It is generally considered one of the best news leads ever written. Wicker and his editors all knew that the active voice is usually much stronger than the passive voice, yet they also knew that this was a time to make the exception. In this particular case, the words "President John Fitzgerald Kennedy" had to be the first four words of the story. It worked.

Good writers know the rules and know when to break them.

Spell Checkers

To be a good news writer, you have to learn how to spell. Spelling is a skill that can be improved with practice. One good technique is to keep a list of words that you have misspelled and work on memorizing their correct spellings. Some people swear by the technique of always looking the words up in a dictionary. Others write their problem words 20 times. Spelling is part of news writing.

What about editors and spelling checkers? Isn't that what editors are for? Isn't that what spelling checkers are for?

No.

Editors are paid to take good, clean copy (stories written with proper spelling, punctuation, grammar, and style) and go over it carefully for the occasional lapse or opportunity for improvement. Anyone who hands an editor copy that is riddled with errors or misspellings will not last long as a professional writer.

Computer software that checks spelling is very handy, but it has serious limitations. One major problem is that it lulls the writer into a false sense of security. Amateur writers may forget that the spelling checker can only see whether a certain combination of letters is a word in the English language. It certainly does not know whether it is the word the writer intended. They are also limited by the ability of the people who wrote the program. A professional news writer should strive to know the language better than that.

An amusing poem that points out the flaws of spelling checkers has been making the rounds of schools, offices, and newsrooms since the early 1990s. I always wondered where it started. After years of trying to locate its source, I found one copy with the name "Dean Zar" written in pencil. A search of the Internet provided the information that Jerrold H. Zar was the dean of the graduate school of Northern Illinois University. He replied to my inquiry with the following message:

"Ah, yes. That poem was transmitted far and wide, appearing in many printed newsletters and, in recent years, on the Internet. It is most often disseminated without attribution, with altered title, or in fractured condition. I formally published the following in 1994. Enjoy!"

—*Jerry Zar*

Candidate for a Pullet Surprise
By Jerrold H. Zar

I have a spelling checker,
It came with my PC.
It plane lee marks four my revue
Miss steaks aye can knot sea.

Eye ran this poem threw it,
Your sure reel glad two no.
Its vary polished in it's weigh.
My checker tolled me sew.

A checker is a bless sing,
It freeze yew lodes of thyme.
It helps me right awl stiles two reed,
And aides me when eye rime.

Each frays come posed up on my screen
Eye trussed too bee a joule.
The checker pours o'er every word
To cheque sum spelling rule.

Bee fore a veiling checker's
Hour spelling mite decline,
And if we're lacks oar have a laps,
We wood bee maid too wine.

Butt now bee cause my spelling
Is checked with such grate flare,
Their are know fault's with in my cite,
Of nun eye am a wear.

Now spelling does knot phase me,
It does knot bring a tier.
My pay purrs awl due glad den
With wrapped word's fare as hear.

To rite with care is quite a feet
Of witch won should bee proud,
And wee mussed dew the best wee can,
Sew flaw's are knot aloud.

Sow ewe can sea why aye dew prays
Such soft wear four pea seas,
And why eye brake in two averse
Buy righting want too pleas.

Dean Zar notes that the title was suggested by Pamela Brown. The poem was based on opening lines suggested by Mark Eckman. By the author's count, 127 of the 225 words of the poem are incorrect (although all words are spelled correctly).

Dr. Jerrold H. Zar is affiliated with the Graduate School, Northern Illinois University, DeKalb, IL 60115-2864.

This poem was first published in the *Journal of Irreproducible Results,* January–February 1994, page 13. Reprinted ("by popular demand") in the *Journal of Irreproducible Results,* Vol. 45, No. 5–6, 2000, page 20. *Journal of Irreproducible Results,* P.O. Box 234, Chicago Heights, IL 60411 USA. Phone: 708-747-3717 Fax: 708-747-3657 E-mail: jir@interaccess.com.

In addition to spelling checkers, most computer software includes grammar and style checkers. They both have the same weaknesses as spelling checkers. English grammar simply is not rational enough to be reduced to a computer program.

If you have a problem with slipping into the passive voice, it may be useful to let the computer check for that weakness. However, do not follow the computer's advice blindly. A good understanding of grammar and style is better than a computer program any day.

How to Write a News Story in 15 Steps

1. FIRST, SELECT A NEWSWORTHY STORY. YOUR GOAL IS TO GIVE A TIMELY ACCOUNT OF A RECENT, INTERESTING, AND SIGNIFICANT EVENT OR DEVELOPMENT

You might report on an event that just took place, preview something that is going to happen soon, explain a recent trend or phenomenon, or feature an interesting person, place, or situation. Chapter 1 discusses characteristics that make a story newsworthy.

Remember that just because something is interesting to you does not mean that it is interesting to everybody. Picture the members of your audience, and try to figure out what will interest them. If your story tells them something new that will affect their lives, chances are that you have a good news story.

Find out what your editor wants. Almost all news stories are written for an editor (or radio or television news director or Internet content manager). Those people are experts on the needs of their particular medium. Learning to work with your editor is an important part of news writing.

However, if an editor gives you a story, and you don't see what is newsworthy about it, you have a problem to solve. If, for example, you are assigned to do a preview of the upcoming county fair, you may be discouraged at getting such a routine assignment. What is the news in something that happens every year? However, you can find out what is new and different about the fair this year. Will there be any changes in the things that most affect the readers, such as price, parking, traffic, and hours?

2. THINK ABOUT YOUR GOALS AND OBJECTIVES IN WRITING THE STORY. WHAT WILL THE READERS WANT AND NEED TO KNOW ABOUT THE SUBJECT? HOW CAN YOU BEST TELL THE STORY?

Good writers always stop to consider their goals and objectives before writing. You can't find the best way to get somewhere if you don't know where you are going. Always consider the readers' point of view. The typical readers may not have as much background information on the subject as you do, so you have to figure out the best way to supply that background without bogging down the story. Also consider what information you should omit. You may have some fascinating information that you are dying to use, but if it does not advance your purpose, don't put it in the story.

In the county fair story, for example, the fair organizers may be excited about a new computer system they use in their office to assign exhibitors to booths, but the computer system may not affect the average reader directly, so it may not be important. (Although a separate feature about how the fair is going high tech could add a touch of irony if most people associate the fair with prize-winning pigs and petunias.)

3. FIND OUT WHO CAN PROVIDE THE MOST ACCURATE INFORMATION ABOUT THE SUBJECT AND HOW TO CONTACT THAT PERSON. FIND OUT WHAT OTHER SOURCES YOU CAN USE TO OBTAIN RELEVANT INFORMATION

Almost every news story will require that the reporter interview people to obtain information. Secondhand facts, hearsay, or information already published elsewhere is unacceptable. Therefore, a reporter finds *sources*—people who can provide firsthand information about news.

A useful technique is to start with someone you know, and ask that person to suggest another person who knows something about the story. Then keep repeating that process until you have all the information you need or all you can get before deadline.

Remember that public officials and recognized experts are not the only good sources. Ordinary people who are not quoted in the media often can make great sources. Neighbors of the controversial power plant, childhood friends of the celebrity, bus drivers in the changing neighborhood, or support personnel at the closing factory are examples of people who can provide a perspective different from that of the officials quoted more commonly.

Besides people, other good sources include such things as documents, reports, and records, which may be available in printed or digital form. Some of the digital information may be posted on the Internet, but others may be available only by request.

In the county fair example, the fair organizing committee is one obvious source, but a youngster who won a blue ribbon in the horse show last year may be planning on trying again this year. An interview with that youngster could prove interesting. If there are neighbors who dread the traffic and congestion, they might provide another side to the story.

4. DO YOUR HOMEWORK. RESEARCH SO THAT YOU HAVE A BASIC UNDERSTANDING OF THE SITUATION BEFORE INTERVIEWING ANYONE ABOUT IT. CHECK CLIPS OF STORIES ALREADY WRITTEN ON THE SUBJECT

"Do your homework" is a basic tenet of journalism. Editors send reporters off to do stories on a wide variety of subjects, and nobody can be an expert on every subject. Thus reporters become experts on acquiring background information quickly.

A newspaper's library of previously published stories traditionally is called the *morgue,* although that term seems to be dying out as libraries move to digital form.

The morgue is a valuable source of information for reporters. Knowing what has already been published on the subject is a good first step in deciding what needs to be written next. The Internet, of course, is also a collection of information that is easily accessible, although the quality and accuracy of the information are variable.

Before interviewing a source, see if you can find some basic biographic information about that person. At the very least, tossing out a line like, "I understand you went to Penn State," for example, might make an interview go more smoothly. It will show the person you made the effort to learn something about him or her. It is also possible that doing your homework before an interview will uncover some crucial information that will unlock a major news story.

Before previewing the county fair, it would be a good idea to read stories from previous years. Then you could ask the committee if the same vendors are coming back and the same events are planned.

5. PREPARE A LIST OF QUESTIONS TO ASK ABOUT THE STORY

A list of prepared questions is essential for a successful interview. It is difficult to keep in mind all the questions you want to ask, and the give-and-take that takes place during an interview is bound to confuse things. So you want to be able to refer to your list and say, "One more question. . . ."

This does not mean that you should be bound slavishly to the list. If the conversation suggests other questions, a good reporter always will follow that train of thought. It is also important to listen carefully to every answer and make sure that you understand it before moving on. Never be afraid to ask someone to repeat, explain, or amplify an answer. Sources appreciate it when a reporter asks them to repeat something. It shows that the reporter cares about getting it right.

If you had prepared a list of questions about the county fair's agricultural events and the source mentions in passing that the hog judging will be held in the barn behind the new Internet café, you might want to stop and ask about the Internet café.

6. ARRANGE TO GET THE NEEDED INFORMATION. THIS MAY MEAN SCHEDULING AN INTERVIEW OR LOCATING THE APPROPRIATE PEOPLE TO INTERVIEW

This step can be as simple as looking up a number in a phone book and calling a person for a telephone interview. In other cases it may require scheduling an in-person interview through an official's assistant. Remember, it may take a while to set up an interview; sources are not always available at a moment's notice.

Generally, an in-person interview is the best choice because you can see the person's expression, mannerisms, and environment. A telephone interview is the second choice and is certainly preferable when time is short. E-mail interviews can be used in a pinch, but people respond to e-mail questions differently than they would in person. Some officials may request that you mail them questions to which they can respond in writing. This situation causes long delays and results in awkward-sounding responses.

If you want to interview the director of the county fair, don't expect to get an interview a few days before the fair begins. This is bound to be "crunch time" for the director.

Either make arrangements to do the interview earlier, or call the director and say, "I know this is a busy time for you, but could you refer me to someone who might have a few minutes to talk to me about the fair?"

7. INTERVIEW THE SOURCE AND TAKE NOTES. ASK YOUR PREPARED QUESTIONS, PLUS OTHER QUESTIONS THAT COME UP IN THE COURSE OF THE CONVERSATION. ASK THE SOURCE TO SUGGEST OTHER SOURCES. ASK IF YOU MAY CALL THE SOURCE BACK FOR FURTHER QUESTIONS LATER

Chapter 16 discusses the art of the interview. Some key concepts in interviewing are things you learned in kindergarten: Show up on time. Smile and be polite. Say "please" and "thank you." Be friendly and courteous while remaining professional. Don't hesitate to ask for an explanation if you don't understand something.

Before leaving the interview, make sure that you have the source's telephone number and the exact spelling of his or her name and title. Even if you are sure that you have it right, it will reassure the source if you double-check.

In the case of the fair director, you might want to say, "What is the best way to contact you after the fair begins?" Some people may be willing to give you a cell phone number, but others may not. Most media-relations professionals will make their cell phone numbers available, but many busy executives will not want to give out their cell phone numbers to reporters.

8. INTERVIEW SECOND AND THIRD SOURCES, ASK FOLLOW-UP QUESTIONS, AND DO FURTHER RESEARCH UNTIL YOU HAVE A GOOD UNDERSTANDING OF THE STORY

A one-source story is inherently weak. Interviewing a second source provides another voice in your story, which is good. It also can alert you to things the first source may have left out or confirm things the first source said.

Sometimes there is only one source, but always try to think of a second. If, for example, you are writing about a serious automobile accident and the police don't know if the injured driver was wearing a seat belt, try finding a firefighter who was on the scene.

9. ASK YOURSELF, "WHAT'S THE STORY?" AND "WHAT'S THE POINT?" BE SURE YOU HAVE A CLEAR FOCUS IN YOUR MIND BEFORE YOU START WRITING. ROUGH OUT A LEAD IN YOUR HEAD

After researching and before writing the story, take a few minutes to make sure that you know your focus. You may have a vast array of material on a variety of subjects. You need to select one, clear focus and stick to that. Your focus statement should be something that you can state in one simple sentence. Preferably it should be a declarative sentence in the active voice and be shorter than 25 words. This sentence may or may not be your lead. However, it probably will be your "nut graf" and appear within the first few paragraphs. (A "nut graf" is a paragraph that summarizes the main point of a news story in a nutshell.)

If you decide to focus on changes to the county fair, for example, your lead might be, "This is not your father's county fair."

10. MAKE A WRITTEN OUTLINE OR PLAN FOR YOUR STORY

Different writers have different techniques for the writing process, but the best writers have some sort of outline or plan. It might be a rough sketch of a few words or an elaborate formal outline. The main benefit of an outline is that you always know where to go next. It is insurance against writer's block. If you finish a sentence and don't know what to write next, simply refer to your plan, and move on to the next point.

If your county fair story is about changes and you have five examples of new things at the fair, jot them down in a list, and move in an organized fashion from one to the next.

11. WRITE YOUR FIRST DRAFT FOLLOWING YOUR PLAN, BUT CHANGING IT AS NECESSARY

Finally, after 10 preliminary steps, you are ready to start writing. If the process of writing suggests things not on your plan, go with the flow, but don't let it carry you too far from your focus.

If the writing proves too difficult, lower your standards. Many successful news writers have suggested plowing through a first draft quickly without worrying too much about perfectly turned phrases or perfect pacing. Being too picky can slow down the writing process, and in news writing, speed is always important.

12. READ THROUGH YOUR FIRST DRAFT LOOKING FOR CONTENT PROBLEMS, HOLES, OR WEAK SPOTS, AND REVISE IT AS NECESSARY. DELETE EXTRA WORDS, SENTENCES, AND PARAGRAPHS. MAKE EVERY WORD COUNT

This is the time to get picky. Check it over word by word. Make sure that every word is correct and necessary. Delete anything that can be deleted without weakening the story. Cast a critical eye on the last paragraph. If you left it for last, perhaps it shouldn't be printed at all. If it is particularly good, perhaps it should be moved up to the beginning of the story.

Be particularly critical of those especially well-turned phrases that just delight you as a writer. There is a good chance that they will draw attention to themselves as creative writing. If they don't serve the purpose of informing the reader, delete them.

13. READ YOUR SECOND DRAFT ALOUD, LISTENING FOR PROBLEMS IN LOGIC OR SYNTAX

Read your story aloud. Really. There is no better way to find mistakes than reading a story out loud.

If you find yourself stumbling over a sentence because it is long and complicated, the reader will too. Typos and misspellings seem to be more visible when you are reading out loud. Somehow when you are reading silently, you tend to skip over words because you know what is coming up. Students and amateurs are too embarrassed to do it, but the best professional writers read their work aloud all the time.

> At one of my first reporting jobs I was too embarrassed to read my story aloud in the middle of the newsroom, so I went into the men's room.
>
> Halfway through the story, I heard the booming bass voice of my boss coming from the next stall.
>
> "What the hell are you doing, Kershner?"
>
> "Uh, reading my story?"
>
> "I know that, but why here?" he asked.

14. COPYEDIT YOUR STORY, CHECKING CAREFULLY FOR SPELLING, PUNCTUATION, GRAMMAR, AND STYLE PROBLEMS

No, this is not what copy editors are for. Professional copy editors expect professional reporters to have checked their own stories before turning them in. Editors dealing with freelance writers learn quickly which freelance writers copyedit their own stories. If you know you have problems with commas, for example, learn the proper uses of a comma (see Chapter 9), and then study every comma in your story.

If you have the luxury of asking someone else to proofread your story, this is the time to do it.

15. DELIVER YOUR FINISHED STORY TO THE EDITOR BEFORE DEADLINE

This is the most important step. No matter how good the story is, if it is late, it is worthless.

How to Write a Strong Lead

1. IN NEWS WRITING, A LEAD IS THE BEGINNING OF A NEWS STORY

The *lead* (pronounced "leed") is the most important part of any news story. It can be the first sentence, the first paragraph, or the first two or three paragraphs of a story. Simple news stories generally have simple leads, which typically consist of a one-sentence paragraph.

Newspaper readers tend to look at photographs first and then scan the headlines, looking for something that interests them. If a headline catches their eyes, they will read the beginning of the news story. If the lead is interesting, they keep reading; if not, they move on to something else.

2. GET RIGHT TO THE POINT. NEWS STORIES DO NOT HAVE INTRODUCTIONS

Many types of writing have introductions; news stories do not. An introduction slowly warms up the reader before getting to the heart of the matter. There is no time for that in news writing. The heart of the matter should be stated clearly in the lead.

3. A GOOD LEAD SUMMARIZES THE MAIN FOCUS OF THE NEWS STORY AND LETS THE READER KNOW WHAT TO EXPECT FROM THE REST OF THE STORY

In addition to summarizing the story, a good lead also may hint at what is to come. This can be done through various techniques, but usually a word or two will suffice. Consider the following lead:

> A homeless man was killed in a Plymouth building fire last night that authorities called suspicious.

All the basic facts are there: who, what, where, why, when, and how. But the details need to be fleshed out. A reader who is interested in the plight of the homeless, in suspicious fires, or in the town of Plymouth will want to read on. The following paragraphs will need to identify the man, identify the specific building, describe the extent of the fire, explain the exact time sequence of events, identify the authorities who are investigating it, and explain what they suspect caused it.

4. A GOOD LEAD USUALLY SHOULD BE LESS THAN 25 WORDS, ALTHOUGH SPECIAL TYPES OF LEADS CAN BE LONGER, IF NECESSARY

In general, shorter sentences are easier to read than longer ones. In *The Associated Press Guide to News Writing*, Renee J. Cappon writes, "Whenever the average sentence length climbs to 20 words or more, many readers are in trouble."

This rule applies primarily to the simple summary lead on a basic hard news story. Some stories, however, may require a more complicated type of lead that will be longer than 25 words. A good writer will know when to follow this rule and when to break it for a good reason.

5. TO DECIDE ON A LEAD, FIRST ASK YOURSELF WHAT THE STORY IS ABOUT. ANSWER THE QUESTION AS IF YOU WERE TELLING A FRIEND WHO HAD NO PRIOR INFORMATION ON THE SUBJECT

Imagine that you work all day in a newsroom, finish an important news story, and go home to your spouse, roommate, friend, parent, or child. This person—more out of courtesy than genuine interest—asks what you wrote about. You are certainly not going to recount every detail of the story, but you want to let this person know the main idea. That should be your lead.

> Four people died in a head-on accident on South Main Street this morning.
> Taxes will go up for residents of the Dennis-Yarmouth School District next year.
> A Tucson girl won a national science competition last week with an experiment on low-water farming.

You could imagine saying these sentences to a friend over dinner, and they would make good leads for news stories.

6. MOST LEADS WILL ANSWER THE BASIC "FIVE-W" QUESTIONS: WHO, WHAT, WHERE, WHEN, WHY, AND HOW

The "five W's" have been a mainstay of news writing for decades. (*Who, what, where, when,* and *why* are the big five, and journalists grant *how* an honorary membership.) It may be impossible to get the answers to all six questions in a short lead, but the attempt to do so will lead a reporter in the right direction. Then decide which elements are most important for a given story and which elements can be left to subsequent paragraphs.

The beauty of the "five W's" is that busy reporters can use them as a memory device designed to help write a lead quickly. If you are stuck for a lead, try running through the basic questions—who, what, where, when, why, and how—and write the lead based on the answers.

7. IN MOST CASES, A LEAD SHOULD BE ONE SIMPLE DECLARATIVE SENTENCE IN ACTIVE VOICE

The sentence pattern that is easiest for people to understand is the basic subject-verb-object pattern. If it is possible to write a lead in this form, that's great. The simple sentence was not created artificially; it is just a description of the way the human mind processes information. Something did something to something. If you can phrase your lead in this way, do so.

When transitive verbs are used in the active voice, it means that the subject performs the action of the verb, and the object receives the action of the verb. This is the most natural sentence pattern, so readers breeze through these sentences easily. A complete discussion of active voice appears in Chapter 11.

8. THE PRIMARY TYPES OF LEADS INCLUDE THE STRAIGHT NEWS (OR SUMMARY) LEAD, THE QUOTE LEAD, THE ANECDOTE LEAD, THE LIST (OR "BAM-BAM-BAM") LEAD, THE DESCRIPTIVE (OR SCENE-SETTING) LEAD, AND THE QUESTION LEAD

The *straight news lead* is also known as the *hard news lead* or the *summary lead*. It is the classic lead in journalism; it is most common and most useful. When in doubt, you can't go wrong with this type of lead. It simply summarizes briefly the story in one sentence. It is the lead used most commonly on a news story written in the inverted-pyramid structure, which is the most common structure (see Chapter 15).

> Taxes will go up for homeowners in Mount Holly Springs next year.

The *quote lead* is a lead that begins with a good, strong quotation. These should be used sparingly and only when the quote is especially good. Occasionally, however, when you have a quotation that is interesting, succinct, and gets the reader into the story quickly, start off with the quote. The quote must be followed by an explanation of how it relates to the story, so the second paragraph is usually very similar to a straight news lead.

> "It was a hell of a melee," said Dean of Students John McIntyre.
>
> McIntyre was discussing a brawl that erupted on the Lafayette College campus last night, after two students got into an argument about smoking. Nine students were injured before campus police broke up the fight.

The *anecdote lead* is a lead that begins with a short vignette or story that sheds light on the subject of the story. Like quotes, these should be used only when the anecdote is exceptionally telling. The anecdotes, of course, must be completely accurate. As much as you might want to make up an anecdote that perfectly demonstrates the main point of the story, fiction has no place in news writing. Like the quote lead, the anecdote must be followed by an explanation of how it relates to the story, so the second paragraph is usually very similar to a straight news lead.

> Mary Silva was pushing her 2-year-old daughter, Tiffany, in a stroller through Riverside Park yesterday afternoon. The toddler was practicing new words she had learned. She pointed out "tree" and "truck" and "flower" much to her mom's delight.
>
> Then Tiffany said "dog!"
>
> But the animal she saw was not a dog; it was a coyote.
>
> A rapid increase in sightings of coyotes in the city has wildlife officials, pet owners and parents concerned.

The *list lead* is a very effective technique for starting a story if you have three examples of people, places, or events that demonstrate the main thrust of the story. Three seems to be the best number for such a list, although two, four, or five could work in some circumstances.

This can be called the "bam-bam-bam" lead because it hammers home the main idea of the story in three quick hits. The three hits must be short, simple, and expressed in parallel form.

> A freshman died of alcohol poisoning after a homecoming party at Adams College.
>
> A sophomore died in an alcohol-related car crash after a fraternity party at Blackstone College.
>
> A senior plunged to his death after drinking a bottle of vodka at an off-campus party at Cleveland College.
>
> These three events, all within the last six months, have brought the problem of college alcohol abuse to the public's attention.

The *descriptive lead* is a lead that sets a scene or paints a picture of a place or situation. It must be interesting enough to get and hold the readers' attention until the summary paragraph, which must follow close on its heels. Merely describing a scene is not enough. There must be elements in the scene described that foreshadow the crux of the story. If you mention that a man is sitting at his desk with pictures of his family nearby, that detail should relate to something in the story, such as his relationship with his family.

> Police Chief David Johnson sits quietly in his backyard in a residential neighborhood on the north side of town. A gentle breeze rustles the leaves on the tall bamboo plants behind the low stone bench where he is sitting. Red and gold koi fish swim in the small fishpond at his feet. His position is similar to that of the seated Buddha in the statue across the pond from his bench.
>
> "I like to sit and meditate here," says Johnson, who may be the only Buddhist police chief in West Virginia.

The *question lead* is—obviously—a question. There is one very important rule about question leads: They must be followed quickly by the answer. There is nothing more frustrating for a reader than reading a question lead and not finding the answer in the story.

The question should not be directed at the reader. Questions that begin, "Have you ever wondered, . . ." run the risk of receiving a negative answer. Don't give the reader the chance to say, "No, not me," and turn the page.

But if you ask and answer an interesting question, it just might work.

> What's the oldest house on Cape Cod?
>
> The Hoxie House, the oldest house on Cape Cod, was built in 1675 for the Rev. John Smith, his wife Susanna and their 13 children.
>
> A proposal to spend $1.5 million to restore and preserve the house will go before residents at town meeting next week.

9. A "NUT GRAF" IS A PARAGRAPH THAT SUMMARIZES IN A NUTSHELL THE MAIN POINT OF THE STORY. IN SIMPLE STORIES, THE LEAD IS THE "NUT GRAF." IN FEATURE STORIES, THE "NUT GRAF" MAY FOLLOW THE LEAD. EVERY NEWS STORY SHOULD HAVE A "NUT GRAF" SOMEWHERE NEAR THE BEGINNING

In the 1950s, the editors of the *Wall Street Journal* issued a memo to their reporters outlining a technique for feature stories that has become known as the *Wall Street Journal* structure. According to Carole Rich's book, *Writing and Reporting News,* the memo said that the stories should have one main point that is put into a "one- or two-paragraph nutshell summary high up in the story."

Over the years, journalists have referred to the idea of a "nutshell summary paragraph," shortening it to "nutshell paragraph," "nutshell graph," and eventually, "nut graf."

10. NEVER BURY THE LEAD

A *buried lead* is a serious error in news writing. To bury the lead is to put the most important element of a story anywhere other than at the beginning. No good reporter would ever commit this crime purposely, but many reporters rush into a story without thinking carefully about the best lead. The error becomes apparent when someone else—usually the editor—sees an element down deep in the story that is more interesting, significant, or newsworthy than what has come before. This is when the editor accuses the reporter of "burying the lead."

11. AVOID LEADS THAT PLACE READERS IN UNLIKELY SITUATIONS

Inexperienced writers occasionally try to put the reader in the picture with the use of second-person-voice writing using the word *you*. This rarely works well. Sometimes it is ridiculous. A lead that begins, "You are backpacking across Antarctica and encounter killer penguins," will not produce a sense of familiarity in many readers. Even more ordinary situations, such as "Your child asks you for help with a science fair project," will fall flat with any reader who does not happen to have a child in school. A stronger lead would be something like, "On-line assistance is now available for parents whose children ask them for help with science fair projects."

12. AVOID CLICHÉ LEADS

It's tempting to say that clichés should be *avoided like the plague*. A cliché is a phrase, usually a metaphor, simile, or aphorism, that has been weakened by overuse.

The ability to spot a cliché *separates the men from the boys*. This *flies in the face* of the idea that a cliché is *worth its weight in gold*. Remember that *brevity is the soul of wit, no news is good news, a picture is worth a thousand words,* and *what goes around comes around.*

If you are tempted to use phrases like these in your news story, don't. Instead, try to think of a new and different phrase that more accurately and more vividly captures the essence of your unique story.

> When I worked at the Evening Sentinel in Carlisle, Pa., in 1978, the editor encouraged short leads by giving an award called "the lead log" to the reporter who wrote the shortest lead of the week. It was just a stick, but I wanted to win it.
>
> I covered a meeting of the South Middletown Township Board of Supervisors, at which a local resident complained that some work the town did on the Yellow Breeches Creek caused his backyard to flood. The board of supervisors decided to take a field trip and look at the resident's backyard themselves. My lead-log–award-winning lead had only two words:
>
> "Muddy shoes."
>
> Of course, I had to go on to say, "That's what the South Middletown Township supervisors got when they investigated a resident's complaint last night." So the whole lead was longer than two words. But the editor only counted the first paragraph, so I won on a technicality.

How to Structure a News Story

1. THE STRUCTURE OF A NEWS STORY IS THE PATTERN OF DEVELOPMENT THAT DETERMINES THE ORDER AND PLACEMENT OF THE ELEMENTS OR PARTS OF THE STORY

Although readers may not be consciously aware of a story's structure, they will be more likely to read a story that has a clear structure. Good journalists plan their stories by making some sort of outline to ensure that the story is well organized. Most news stories have too many points to be presented in random order. Placing the elements in the best order makes stories readable and interesting.

A story with a clear and organized structure gives a sense of security to the reader, just as a building with a clear structure appears more stable or a piece of music with a consistent beat sounds more pleasant.

Using a planned structure is also helpful for the writer. Spending a few minutes at the start of the writing process to plan a structure saves lots of time later on. A writer following a structure can see easily what to write next.

2. EVERY NEWS STORY SHOULD HAVE A CLEAR AND OBVIOUS STRUCTURE

Whether it is a long feature story or a short news brief, a news story should have some pattern of development. The important thing is to avoid writing a story that jumps from one point to another with no clear sense of direction or order.

Experienced writers may end up creating a structure with little or no forethought, but most writers have to take a few minutes to decide on a plan of action. A writer can select from one of the common patterns that are used frequently or invent a new one to suit the content. Some common structures include the classic inverted pyramid, the champagne-glass structure, the *Wall Street Journal* style, and the multiple-element structure.

3. THE CLASSIC STRUCTURE FOR MOST NEWS STORIES IS CALLED THE INVERTED-PYRAMID STRUCTURE

Picture a pyramid standing on its point, with the broad base at the top. It may not sound very stable, but it has been used since the time of the Civil War to describe the most common way to write a news story. The point of the metaphor is that the first sentence in the story is the broadest, most general, and most important part of the news story. Everything else in the story is based on that first sentence. This is analogous to the base of the pyramid. In architecture it is on the bottom, but in news writing it is at the "top of the story." In both cases, it is built first.

In an inverted-pyramid news story, the lead, the "nut graf," and the main point of the story are all in the same sentence, and that sentence comes first. It is broad enough that everything else in the story relates to that first sentence. A reader should be able to read that first sentence and know what the story is all about. Based on that one sentence, the reader may choose to move on to another story, and frequently, that is exactly what readers do.

Some historians say that the inverted-pyramid structure developed when Civil War correspondents began sending stories to their home papers via telegraph. Sometimes soldiers cut telegraph lines to disrupt communications, so editors instructed the reporters to put the results of the battles in the first paragraphs of the stories.

Another theory is that reporters began copying news summaries issued by the United States War Department, which adopted a style of summarizing the most important results in the first paragraphs because busy government officials did not have time to read the entire reports. In any case, the inverted-pyramid structure is a technique that is valued by newspaper editors who have more copy than space and have to cut stories. In the inverted-pyramid style, stories can be cut from the end without depriving readers of important information.

In the twenty-first century, the same technique is valued on the Internet, where readers are looking for quick summaries of stories without needing to scroll down.

4. IN A SENSE, THE INVERTED-PYRAMID STRUCTURE TELLS THE STORY BACKWARDS

Sometimes, the inverted-pyramid story is explained as a story in which the end of the story is told first. For example, a typical news story about a house fire might begin

> Six people were left homeless when fire destroyed their two-story wood frame home in Goleta last night.
> The cause of the fire is under investigation, but firefighters on the scene said an unattended candle in one of the second-floor bedrooms may have ignited drapery.
> The family made arrangements to stay with relatives in Santa Barbara.

The fact that the family lost their home was one of the last things to happen in this news event. If the story were told chronologically, it might begin

> Mary Donahue, 16, of Goleta, was doing homework in her bedroom at about 7 p.m. yesterday when she decided to light the scented candle her Aunt Barbara had given her for Christmas. She placed it on the windowsill, where a gentle breeze carried the bayberry scent through her room. A few minutes later, her boyfriend, Bob, called and asked her to meet him at the library so they could study together. Forgetting about the candle, she headed for the library . . .

This version would be fine in a short story or perhaps even as an anecdote to begin a long feature story about fire safety. For a short, simple news story, however, readers expect to get the results first. This is what the inverted-pyramid structure does—it starts with the bottom line.

If the story is about a three-hour city council meeting at which the council decided (just before adjournment) to raise taxes, that last-minute decision becomes the lead.

The fact that the council president called the meeting to order and that the secretary read the minutes of the previous meeting may have come first at the meeting, but they certainly do not come first in the news story.

Whatever is most important to the readers becomes the base of the pyramid and comes first in the story. Everything else becomes a supporting detail.

5. THE INVERTED-PYRAMID STRUCTURE PLACES FACTS IN DESCENDING ORDER OF IMPORTANCE

The rest of the story in the inverted-pyramid structure simply adds supporting facts and details in descending order of importance. Thanks to word-processing software, reporters can type separate paragraphs about each detail worthy of inclusion in the story and then move them into the order of importance.

As recently as the 1980s, copy editors and reporters would type long stories on long rolls of paper and then literally cut them with scissors and paste them with rubber cement into different orders. Fortunately, it is now much easier to cut and paste paragraphs on a computer without getting rubber cement all over your desk.

6. WHEN YOU RUN OUT OF INTERESTING THINGS TO SAY, STOP WRITING

After arranging things in descending order of importance, look at the last few items with a critical eye. If they are not interesting or important, delete them. Stories written in the inverted-pyramid structure do not have endings.

How do you end a news story written this way?

Stop typing.

7. FEATURE STORIES ARE MORE LIKELY TO USE STRUCTURES OTHER THAN THE INVERTED-PYRAMID STRUCTURE

Feature stories must have something to grab and hold the reader's interest other than the newsworthiness associated with hard news stories. To "feature" something is to draw attention to it. A good feature story draws attention to something interesting by use of exceptional writing. Good ways to heighten interest in feature stories include literary techniques such as irony, contrast, drama, suspense, and dialogue. Feature writing often involves storytelling. Chapter 24 discusses feature stories in greater detail.

8. THE HOURGLASS OR CHAMPAGNE-GLASS STRUCTURE USES A CHRONOLOGICAL STORYTELLING TECHNIQUE

In contrast to the inverted-pyramid structure, the champagne-glass structure does include a chronological section. Picture a champagne glass with a wide, fluted bowl at the top, a long, narrow stem with bubbles rising through it, and a wide, flat base at the bottom. The story begins, like an inverted pyramid, with a summary lead explaining the whole story. Then the writer includes a chronology of events in order (represented by the stem of the glass) and finally returns to a general summary at the end of the story.

This is most often found in a feature story or a story that is suited to a narrative technique. If you find yourself saying, "It's an interesting story. Here is how it happened," you should consider such a narrative technique. For example, a routine housebreaking story could be made into an interesting feature story if there is an interesting story behind the events:

> A rotisserie-cooked chicken led to the arrest of a Johnstown youth on charges of breaking and entering last night. The 16-year-old boy, whose name was withheld by police because of his age, will be brought before a juvenile court judge Monday.
>
> According to police, here is how the cooked-chicken caper was cracked:
>
> William and Mary Sorvino of Elm Street decided to go out to dinner last night at the Red Lobster in Milford. When they arrived home about 8 p.m., they found their house in disarray. Drawers and cabinets were open, and their TV had been dropped just inside the front door, as if quickly abandoned by a burglar. The kitchen door looked like it had been forced open, and the kitchen was a mess. There was a half-eaten rotisserie-roasted chicken sitting in its plastic tray on the kitchen table.
>
> The Sorvinos called the Johnstown Police, who dispatched two officers, Margaret Powers and James Delahunt. After inspecting the mess, they commented on the half-eaten chicken. It was still warm. Powers asked if it had come from their refrigerator.
>
> "No," said Mrs. Sorvino, "I don't know where it came from."
>
> "I think I do," said Powers. "They sell chickens like that at the convenience store up the street."
>
> The officers went to the QuickStop Market on Elm Street and asked if they had sold any roasted chickens lately.
>
> "Just one," said the manager. He said he remembered the purchaser because he was the son of a regular customer. The boy had been coming into the shop for years, usually with his mother.
>
> The manager told the police the youth appeared to have been intoxicated, and the manager was worried the kid was going to drive. He was relieved to see the youth was on foot.
>
> "He just put the chicken under his arm and staggered on down Elm Street," the manager told Officer Powers. The manager provided the police with the name and address of the youth's mother. . . .

The ending of the story would go back to provide more general information about the nature of the arrest and charges.

9. THE WALL STREET JOURNAL STRUCTURE BEGINS WITH A SOFT LEAD FOLLOWED BY A "NUT GRAF," SUPPORTING POINTS, AND AN ENDING THAT REFERS TO THE LEAD

The *Wall Street Journal* is one of the best-selling newspapers in the world. Usually there is a feature story in the center column of the front page that puts a human face on a major issue. Most of these stories follow a tried-and-true structure that has been imitated widely in newspapers all over the world.

Such stories begin with an anecdote about one individual or one family. This anecdote illustrates one example of a general trend or issue, which is explained in a "nut graf" that follows close on the heels of the anecdote. Then there is a series of facts, quotes, and documentation to back up the "nut graf." The story ends with a second reference to the anecdote in the lead.

The concept of an ending that echoes the beginning of the story is sometimes called a "circle kicker." It is a technique that can work effectively in feature stories, but it should be used with caution. A writer must remember that newspaper readers may not get to the end of a story. If you want to be sure the reader sees a particular fact, quote, or detail, put it near the beginning of the story, not at the end.

10. MULTIPLE-ELEMENT STORIES MENTION SEVERAL ELEMENTS IN THE LEAD AND COVER EACH IN A SEPARATE SECTION OF THE STORY

Any good piece of writing should have only one main point. Sometimes, however, circumstances require that a news story cover several related elements. For example, if a reporter covers a meeting of a governmental board, and the board takes three important actions, it may be necessary to mention all three in the lead of the story. In such a case, the one main point of the story is that the board appointed three people to important positions.

Therefore, the lead could say that the board of trustees filled three positions yesterday and mention the names and positions of all three. Then, in a multiple-element story, the reporter would write several paragraphs about the first appointment, then several paragraphs about the second appointment, and then several paragraphs about the third appointment. General facts that apply to all three elements can go at the end.

One way to visualize the structure of this story is to think of it as a story about apples, oranges, and bananas:

1. Apples, oranges, and bananas
2. Apples
3. Apples
4. Apples
5. Oranges
6. Oranges
7. Oranges
8. Bananas
9. Bananas
10. Bananas
11. Apples, oranges, and bananas

11. MOST FEATURE STORIES HAVE A BEGINNING, A MIDDLE, AND AN ENDING

If the story lends itself to feature-writing techniques, like the roasted chicken story earlier, it probably will need to have a clear beginning, middle, and end. This contrasts with hard news stories written in the inverted-pyramid style, which do not have an explicit beginning, middle, and end.

News stories hold readers' interest by virtue of their inherent newsworthiness. Because of this, readers are likely to stop reading at any point where they have satisfied their curiosity. But feature stories hold readers' interest with excellent writing. Theoretically, it is more likely that the readers will continue to the end.

12. CONSIDER BREAKING OUT PART OF THE STORY TO A SIDEBAR OR BOX

A *sidebar* is a small companion story that is placed beside the main story in a newspaper, magazine, or other medium. If there is some information that would be useful to the reader but does not fit easily into the structure of the main story, it might be a good idea to write it as a separate story. Sidebars must be short—usually less than 100 words. This is so because they are used to attract readers who are not interested in reading long stories. Boxes, fact boxes, factoids, "infographics," and similar items are even shorter items that are essentially graphic devices to catch readers' attention.

13. LET THE CONTENT OF THE STORY DETERMINE THE STRUCTURE

Just as graphic elements should serve the content of the story, the internal structure of the story should be content-based. In other words, use the structure that best tells the story. Do not become enamored of a particular structure and try to force a story into it. If you have a great anecdote that perfectly illustrates a general trend, consider the *Wall Street Journal* structure. If you have an interesting tale that lends itself to chronological storytelling, consider the champagne-glass structure. If you have a single-element, straightforward, hard news story, stick with the inverted pyramid.

14. GOOD QUOTES GIVE LIFE TO A STORY

Whatever structure you choose for your story, be sure to include quotations. Good quotes liven up a story the same way dialogue livens up a piece of fiction or an interview livens up a television report.

If possible, get a quote into the first three paragraphs of a story. The quote provides a second voice for the story, besides the voice of the reporter. Look for a quote that explains the main point of the story in different words from those already in the lead.

Content always should be your guide, but try to use a quote every three or four paragraphs, if possible.

15. ALWAYS CONSIDER DELETING THE LAST PARAGRAPH

Almost any story can be improved by shortening. Readers do not have time to read excess verbiage. Shorter is almost always better.

There are three good reasons to consider deleting the last paragraph of any news story. First, if the story is in the inverted-pyramid style and you have placed details in descending order of importance, the last paragraph is likely to be insignificant. Second, if the last paragraph is a delightful little kicker that you think is an absolutely wonderful turn of phrase, it is likely to call attention to itself and distract from the main point, which was stated in the lead. Third, if it is a paragraph that just didn't fit anywhere else in the story, chances are that the readers can get along without it.

How to Conduct an Interview

1. THE INTERVIEW IS THE PRIMARY METHOD OF GATHERING INFORMATION FOR NEWS STORIES. PERSONAL INTERVIEWS PROVIDE THE MOST RELIABLE INFORMATION ABOUT RECENT SIGNIFICANT EVENTS

Almost all news writing is the result of one or more interviews. Whereas creative writing can come from one's own thoughts, and academic writing can come from scholarly research, news writing must come from gathering new information, usually from interviews. A reporter may read other publications for background information, but information that has already been published elsewhere will not be news.

If you are just starting a news story, one of the first questions you should ask yourself is, "Whom can I ask about this?" If you find someone who can provide new information about an interesting subject, you have a news story.

2. DO YOUR HOMEWORK. BE SURE THAT YOU KNOW SOME BACKGROUND ABOUT THE SOURCE AND THE SUBJECT BEFORE YOU BEGIN THE INTERVIEW. DON'T WASTE THE SOURCE'S TIME ON BASIC QUESTIONS YOU COULD HAVE ANSWERED EASILY ELSEWHERE

Sometimes a reporter is forced by circumstances to interview someone "cold"—that is, without any preparation. Whenever possible, a reporter will want to do some basic research before the interview. The source will appreciate it because it means that you won't be wasting time with elementary questions that you could have answered with a quick search of the Internet or a reference book such as *Who's Who*. The reporter benefits because it means that the reporter will have more intelligent and more probing questions. So much background is available on the Internet now that there is no excuse for not knowing the background of the person you are interviewing.

For example, there is no need to ask a professor, "Where did you go to college?" That information is in the college catalog. Having checked that, the reporter could move on to a question such as, "I see that you received your master's degree from Harvard and your doctorate from Yale. Given the rivalry between those schools, to which do you feel greater loyalty?"

3. BE POLITE. BEING COURTEOUS DURING AN INTERVIEW IS ONE OF THE BEST WAYS TO GET INFORMATION. REMEMBER THAT YOU ARE ASKING THE SOURCE TO DO YOU A FAVOR BY ANSWERING YOUR QUESTIONS

You can never be too polite. Be sure to thank the source repeatedly for taking the time to talk with you. Even if you dislike the person, be courteous and pleasant. Saying "thank you" a few times is a small price to pay for a good story.

David Brinkley (1920–2003) had a long and distinguished career in journalism, starting with United Press International, a worldwide wire service, and later becoming part of the Huntley-Brinkley team that was one of the most popular TV network newscasts from 1956 to 1970. He hosted a Sunday morning interview show on ABC from 1981 to 1996. When guests appeared on that show, Brinkley always thanked them profusely for coming, and then, after the interviews were over, he always thanked them again, often several times.

"Thank you very much for coming," he would say. "We appreciate it very much. Thank you for taking time from your busy schedule. Thank you. Thank you very much." It sounded almost ridiculous to hear one of America's most distinguished and respected journalists being so effusive in his thanks to a guest who was likely to be much younger than he was. However, on Monday morning the front pages of many newspapers frequently carried a story about some dramatic announcement made the previous morning on *This Week with David Brinkley*. Somewhere between the extensive thanks when the guest arrived and the extensive thanks when the guest departed, David Brinkley managed to squeeze more news out of the source than any other journalist.

Thank you, David Brinkley.

4. SMILE AND BE PLEASANT. IF YOU MAKE THE EXPERIENCE A PLEASANT ONE FOR THE SOURCE, HE OR SHE WILL BE MORE LIKELY TO COOPERATE AND HELP YOU WITH YOUR STORY. IT IS A GOOD IDEA TO COMPLIMENT THE PERSON AND EXCHANGE PLEASANTRIES

Beginning reporters may be nervous when they begin an interview. This is all the more reason for them to smile. Smiling at people relaxes both of you. There is no need to be formal or severe in an interview. Being friendly and complimentary is a good way to put someone at ease. After that, the information flows much more easily.

Before taking out your notebook or tape recorder and getting down to business, it is an excellent idea to exchange small talk.

"What an interesting office; are those pictures of your children?"

Little comments like those can help both of you relax.

5. REQUEST INTERVIEWS AS FAR AHEAD AS POSSIBLE. ALTHOUGH YOU MAY BE FACING A TIGHT DEADLINE, YOU CANNOT EXPECT EVERY SOURCE TO BE ABLE TO DROP EVERYTHING AND ANSWER YOUR QUESTIONS IMMEDIATELY

Sometimes a reporter needs information right away, but if you have a little time, it helps to request an interview in advance. People who are not in the news media are used to setting up business appointments several days in advance. If you have the luxury of doing so, ask the source to schedule an interview at his or her convenience. If it is too far off, you might follow up by saying something like, "I'm sorry, I have a deadline coming up. Is there any way we could talk sooner than that? I would hate to write the story without your comments."

Most reporters are working on several stories at once. Keep a good appointment book, either on paper or on a computer, and keep scheduling appointments for all your stories. In this way, when one gets delayed, there is always another story to work on.

6. INTERVIEW PEOPLE IN PERSON WHENEVER POSSIBLE BECAUSE YOU CAN LEARN A LOT FROM THEIR DEMEANOR, MANNERISMS, DRESS, AND APPEARANCE. IF IT IS POSSIBLE TO INTERVIEW THEM IN THEIR PLACE OF BUSINESS OR HOME, THAT WILL GIVE YOU MORE INFORMATION

There is no substitute for looking in a person's eyes during a conversation. On the one hand, you may get a sense of whether the person is lying. On the other hand, you may get a feeling you can really trust this person. Either way, human beings connect and communicate in person better than through any other means. The in-person interview also can give you a sense of context, especially if you see the source's home or office. Even if the interview is at a neutral place, such as a restaurant, you can see how the source interacts with others around him or her. Is the person rude to the server or compassionate?

That said, most journalists end up doing most interviews over the telephone. It saves so much time that it has become the most common form of interview. A journalist conducting a telephone interview should make the most of it by including a little casual conversation in order to get to know the person better, if possible. Be sure that the source knows that you are a reporter writing a story for publication, and be sure to ask for the proper spelling of the source's name and his or her complete title or affiliation.

If you want to tape-record a telephone interview, be sure to get the person's permission first. It is unethical—and in most jurisdictions illegal—to tape-record a conversation without the permission of all parties involved.

A third choice is an interview by e-mail. Sometimes it is all that is available, but the words typed by someone in an e-mail note do not sound like a conversation. The quotes do not have that familiar pattern of human speech. E-mail interviews do have the advantage of making misquotation much less likely, though.

7. DRESS APPROPRIATELY FOR AN INTERVIEW. WHEN POSSIBLE, TRY TO DRESS IN THE SAME STYLE AND DEGREE OF FORMALITY AS THE PERSON YOU ARE INTERVIEWING

If you were going to interview a bank president, it would be a good idea to wear a business suit. If you are going to interview a farm hand, jeans might be more appropriate. The level of formality people choose for their dress sends signals in society. Without going to extremes, try to dress in a way that will put the source at ease.

Dan Rather, the longtime anchor of the "CBS Evening News," follows this advice. When he goes on the road to interview people, he often dresses very casually when interviewing people who are also dressed casually. However, when he is interviewing government officials and executives, he will show up dressed as they are.

> In 1970 I started a new job as a reporter for the Providence Journal. I had just graduated from college, and during my college days, I usually dressed in bell-bottom jeans and had long hair. I enjoyed rock concerts, and I fit right in with the crowd. But when I got my first professional reporting job, I cut my hair, shaved my beard, and put on a suit and tie. One of my first assignments was to cover a rock concert at the University of Rhode Island. When I showed up at the gate, they took one look at this conservative-looking, overdressed guy in a suit and tie and refused to let me in.

8. TAPE RECORDERS ARE OFTEN MORE HARMFUL THAN HELPFUL. THEY MAKE PEOPLE FEEL AWKWARD, THEY ARE SUBJECT TO MALFUNCTION, AND THEY REQUIRE TRANSCRIPTION AFTER THE INTERVIEW. MOST PROFESSIONAL REPORTERS PREFER WRITTEN NOTES

There are definitely two schools of thought when it comes to using tape or digital recorders. The advantages are that you can play back the recording to make sure that a quote is exactly accurate and that you can listen to the entire interview a second time to see if you missed anything. If there is a question of accuracy later and you have saved the recording, you can use the recording to defend yourself.

In certain unusual circumstances, such as jailhouse interviews with people accused of crimes, interviews in which the reporter thinks there is a high likelihood that the sources are going to incriminate themselves, or contentious circumstances likely to result in lawsuits, a recording might be advisable legally. In such cases, it is a good idea for the reporter to consult with an attorney for legal advice before conducting the interview.

In most situations, the disadvantages of recording outweigh the advantages. Mechanical and technical problems can cause any equipment to fail, so it is unwise to depend on it. Another disadvantage is that you have to listen to it, which can be very time-consuming. When reporters are on tight deadlines they frequently have to write up a story immediately after an interview. There is no time to listen to the recording again.

The biggest disadvantage of recording interviews, however, is that it makes some people uncomfortable. Even when the reporter is taking notes, the interview is still just a conversation between two people. When the recorder is turned on, though, some people clam up. They become so self-conscious about their word choice that they are afraid to say anything.

So the choice made by most reporters is to rely on good notes. This does not mean writing down every word the source says—that would be impossible. It means making note of the important points and pausing to write down sentences and phrases that might make good quotes. Most of all, it means listening carefully to the source's comments so that you really understand the person's point of view.

9. WHEN TAKING NOTES, FEEL FREE TO ASK THE PERSON BEING INTERVIEWED TO SLOW DOWN OR TO REPEAT ANSWERS. SOURCES USUALLY APPRECIATE THAT

When the person you are interviewing says something particularly interesting or quotable, ask him or her to pause. Usually the person will be flattered that you are interested in what he or she had to say. People who are not used to being interviewed by reporters probably will be curious about the process, and they may wonder how their words get turned into news stories. If the reporter says, "That's very interesting; please wait a minute while I get that down," it will reassure them that the reporter is being careful.

Furthermore, if the reporter mentions that a certain phrase would make a good quote and asks the person to repeat it, that makes it much less likely that the person would later claim to have been misquoted.

10. DO NOT WRITE DOWN EVERY WORD THE SOURCE SAYS. IT IS MORE IMPORTANT TO LISTEN THOUGHTFULLY AND MAKE NOTES ABOUT THE MOST IMPORTANT POINTS AND THE BEST QUOTES. READ BACK THE QUOTES YOU EXPECT TO USE

Good listening skills are vital for reporters. In fact, it is more important to be a good listener than to be a good note-taker. If you listen carefully and attentively, you will remember what the source was saying when you write the story. If the person tells a charming story about a beloved childhood pet, it may be enough to listen carefully and think about what the person is saying. Then just write "dog story" in your notebook, and that should be enough to jog your memory. (You may want to ask for a telling detail or two, such as, "What was the dog's name?" and "How old were you at the time?")

If you hear a sentence that would make a good quote, do not hesitate to interrupt the person and say, "Wait a minute. That was great. Let me see if I got that right. You said, 'I think heaven must smell like Hershey, Pa.'? That's terrific."

11. ALWAYS ASK SOURCES IF YOU MAY CALL THEM BACK FOR MORE INFORMATION OR CLARIFICATION LATER, AND ASK FOR TELEPHONE NUMBERS WHERE THEY CAN BE REACHED

Beyond a doubt, the most important question in any interview is, "May I call you back if I have more questions later?" And of course, be sure to ask for a number where you can reach the person. It is very common to get halfway through writing a story and realize that there is a detail you forgot to ask about.

12. ASK THE SOURCE IF HE OR SHE CAN SUGGEST ANOTHER PERSON TO TALK TO ON THE SAME SUBJECT

Make it clear that you appreciate the person's help and that you are not asking for another source because you are not satisfied with his or her answers. Just explain that a good reporter always tries to talk to more than one person on any story, and you would appreciate another name to contact. This second or third voice can be the difference between an adequate story and an excellent story.

13. PREPARE A WRITTEN LIST OF QUESTIONS, BUT BE FLEXIBLE ENOUGH TO ADD NEW QUESTIONS IF THE SOURCE'S ANSWERS SUGGEST THEM. ASK OPEN-ENDED QUESTIONS THAT CANNOT BE ANSWERED BY A SIMPLE "YES" OR "NO"

It is always a good idea to have a list of questions prepared before going into an interview. The questions should be open-ended questions that will prompt complete responses. Instead of asking, "Have you always wanted to be a firefighter?" which could elicit an answer of "yes" or "no," ask something like, "How did you feel about firefighters when you were a child?" If the answer is still too brief, try asking the person to elaborate. "Can you tell me a little more about that?"

Again, listening skills are very important. Listen carefully to the person's answers, and ask questions based on the answers. Let the questions flow naturally wherever the conversation goes, as long as it is related to the subject of the story.

And never pretend to understand an answer if you don't. In the 1970s there was a popular detective show on television called "Columbo." Peter Falk played a detective whose interviewing technique often included "playing dumb."

"Gosh," he would say, stuffing his hands in his wrinkled raincoat, "I'm sorry, I just have one more question. I must be missing something, but I can't understand how your fingerprints could have ended up all over the murder weapon."

The Columbo technique works very well in conducting an interview for a news story. Feel free to plead ignorance and ask the person to explain something again if you don't understand it completely. You will not be able to explain it to your readers, listeners, or viewers if you don't understand it yourself.

14. ALWAYS IDENTIFY YOURSELF AS A REPORTER CONDUCTING AN INTERVIEW FOR PUBLICATION. DO NOT ACCEPT ANY LIMITATIONS, SUCH AS KEEPING INFORMATION SECRET OR "OFF THE RECORD," EXCEPT IN THE RAREST CIRCUMSTANCES

At the beginning of any interview, be sure to make it perfectly clear who you are and what you are doing. Tell the person your name and that you are writing a story for a newspaper, magazine, a radio or television news department, or a blog or Web site. In most situations, it would be unethical to quote someone in a news story if that person did not know that he or she was being interviewed for a news story.

People making speeches or public officials speaking at public meetings, of course, can expect to be quoted, and there is no need to notify them that you intend to do so. Private citizens who may think that they are having a private conversation deserve the courtesy of being told if you plan to quote them in the news media.

Once it is clear that you are working on a news story, then everything is "on the record." Sources may have seen popular films such as *All the Presidents Men* and think that it is routine to "go off the record," but this is not true. In almost all situations a reporter is likely to encounter, everything should be fair game for publication. Reporters are in the business of printing information, not keeping secrets. If someone wants to give you some information "off the record," politely decline the offer and say that you cannot accept those limitations. Most of the time the source will be just as happy to go ahead and allow you to print the information with his or her name attached.

15. ASK THE PEOPLE YOU INTERVIEW IF THERE IS ANYTHING THEY WOULD LIKE TO ADD

Be sure to ask an open-ended question such as, "Is there anything else our readers should know to fully understand this situation?" or "Is there anything you can think of that I neglected to ask about?" It is quite possible that the real news will come not from one of your prepared questions but from something the person volunteers. You never want to be in the position of asking later why they didn't tell you about the secret slush fund and having the person say, "You never asked."

16. NEVER OFFER YOUR OWN OPINIONS AS PART OF AN INTERVIEW

A good reporter acts as a medium, passing along information from the source to the reader, listener, or viewer. A good medium passes along information as free from distortion as possible. Getting into a debate or argument with the source will never help that process. Thus, even if you strongly disagree with the source's point of view, just keep asking questions, and make sure that you can portray that point of view accurately in the story. You probably will want to interview someone else to provide an opposing point of view, but that view should come from another interviewee, not from the reporter.

One day in 1984 I was watching Mr. Rogers' Neighborhood on PBS with my younger son, Brandon. When Mr. Rogers went through the routine of taking off his blazer and putting on his cardigan, I noticed his tie had little images of Nantucket Island on it. As an editor of the Cape Cod Times, which covers Nantucket, I wondered what his connection to the island was. So I called the Pittsburgh station where his show was produced, WQED, and asked to speak with someone connected with the show. I reached a producer and asked about the Nantucket tie. When he told me Mr. Rogers has a summer home on Nantucket, I said I would like to schedule an interview with Mr. Rogers to talk about his connection to the region. I asked when such an interview would be possible.

"How about right now?" he asked.

In about a minute, I heard the familiar soothing tones that I had been hearing on television for years coming out of the telephone receiver.

"Hello, this is Fred Rogers. Can I help you?"

I was completely unprepared for the interview. I never expected it would be so easy to reach the host of the most popular children's television show in America within a matter of minutes.

But, just as he dedicated his life to making children feel comfortable, he spent the conversation making me feel comfortable. He asked about my family and asked for the names of my two sons. A week after the interview, we received two autographed photographs of Mr. Rogers, one inscribed to Brandon and one to his brother, Ben.

How to Cover Meetings and Speeches

1. WHEN COVERING A SPEECH OR MEETING, LOOK FOR ONE MAIN POINT, AND MAKE THAT POINT THE FOCUS OF THE STORY

Some of the most common news writing assignments in journalism involve covering a meeting of a governmental body, a speech, or a press conference. In any of these situations, the reporter is bound to hear much more information than could possibly be included in a news story. The best approach, therefore, is to select one focus, one aspect, or one main point and make that the lead of the news story.

Sometimes other news will be added at the end of the story in a section that begins, "In other business . . ." or "Jones also mentioned. . . ." Most of the story, however, should be devoted to the single most important aspect. This makes for a story that readers will be able to follow.

Do not begin by declaring that the members of the board met or the person spoke. Don't say they met; say what they did. Don't say she spoke; say what she said.

2. REMEMBER THAT YOUR MAIN OBLIGATION IS TO THE READER, SO BASE THE STORY ON WHAT THE READER WILL NEED OR WANT TO KNOW

Just as hostages begin to relate to and sympathize with their captors, reporters begin to feel sympathetic toward the members of a town council, school board, or other governmental body they are covering. After sitting through a long, boring meeting with these people, a reporter may begin to think like them. Thus, if the board of education wants to emphasize to taxpayers that it is considering an "innovative new approach to evaluating curricula," this sounds like the big news, right?

Wrong! At least it would be wrong if the board also decided at the same meeting to increase school taxes, to close a neighborhood school, or to cancel a popular music program.

Remember that public officials, especially those who are elected, often will try to manipulate the media to get the most favorable coverage possible. The reporter's job is to figure out what the general public needs to know and provide them with that information. This may not be the same as the information public officials would like to see emphasized.

3. STAND UP FOR THE RIGHT OF THE GENERAL PUBLIC TO KNOW WHAT THEIR GOVERNMENT IS DOING

Every state of the United States and most jurisdictions in other Western countries have open-meeting laws that prohibit governmental bodies from acting in secret. Reporters, representing the public, have a right to attend any meetings at which decisions are made. There are usually restrictions on when and how closed meetings can be held. There are also freedom-of-information acts on the federal and state levels that make governmental documents available to the public on request. All reporters should be familiar with the laws that govern their jurisdictions and know how to use them. It is important to remember that these laws are designed to provide information to any member of the public; they do not single out reporters for special rights.

This means that reporters have a right to find out what government officials are doing so that they can pass along the information to the public. The public has a right to the information so that they can make informed decisions at the ballot box.

4. FOCUS ON WHATEVER WAS THE MOST IMPORTANT, SIGNIFICANT, OR INTERESTING ASPECT OF THE SPEECH OR MEETING

A story about a speech, meeting, or press conference should begin with the information that is most important to the readers, listeners, or viewers. The story should not begin the same way the event began. A speaker often begins with a little joke, to warm up the audience.

"I just flew in from the Coast, folks. Boy, are my arms tired." (Pause for laughs.) "But seriously, folks, I am pleased to be here, . . . but then at my age I am pleased to be anywhere!" (Pause for laughs.)

Unless the focus of the story is the world's oldest jokes, none of this belongs in a news story. It is possible that the real news may appear at the end of the speech or even in the answer to a question after the speech.

John Smith announced last night that he will not seek reelection as a county commissioner next November.

Smith's surprise announcement came in response to a question at the end of a speech about the importance of reading at the dedication of the new county library.

Smith said he wants to give others an opportunity to serve on the board.

"I think it's time to get some new blood in county government," he said,

"I'm getting too old for all these meetings," added Smith, 68.

5. DO NOT INCLUDE EVERYTHING SAID IN THE MEETING OR SPEECH, JUST THE MOST IMPORTANT PARTS

After sitting through the entire speech or meeting, a reporter is likely to feel a compulsion to include everything that was said. After taking all those notes, it may feel like it would be a shame to leave anything out, but it would serve the readers better to leave out all but the most important information. Ask yourself, "What do the readers need to know?" Focus on the one main point, and then, if necessary, add some other important items, but do not feel obligated to include everything.

6. LOOK FOR THE IMPACT THE EVENT WILL HAVE ON THE READERS, AND EXPLAIN THAT IN THE STORY

A government board may spend a lot of time and effort on something such as bureau-cratic reorganization that is important to those involved but less important to the general public. A reporter always should ask how it will affect the readers.

This principle also applies to the way a decision is phrased. If a board raises taxes, for example, the officials may describe it as an increase of "three mills" or a certain percentage increase. These figures need to be translated into dollars and cents to show their impact on taxpayers. Giving the readers an example can show how the decision will affect them.

The owner of a $100,000 home can expect to pay $989 in real estate tax next year, compared to $898 this year.

Or instead of reporting that a new "communication enhancement system" was approved, the story might say, "residents calling the county courthouse will hear an auto-matic voice-mail system instead of a live operator starting next January."

7. INCLUDE AUDIENCE REACTION AND SETTING IN THE STORY

Did the school board meet in the high school library with five other people present, or did it meet in the auditorium before hundreds of residents? It may be important for the read-ers to know this. Were there a lot of loud boos when the board decided to cancel all school field trips, or was there applause? This supplementary information is rarely the focus of the story, but it can add information that helps readers to understand the context. Occa-sionally, it takes on more importance if, for example, an overflow crowd shows up and the board decided to adjourn to a larger location at a later date.

8. FOLLOW UP AND GET REACTIONS TO THE SPEECH OR MEETING IF APPROPRIATE AND POSSIBLE

Sometimes the news story is due immediately at the end of the speech or meeting, but if there is time, you might be able to get reactions from people affected by the decision or announcement.

Mayor John Washington said this morning he would fight the town council's decision to cut his staff "by any means necessary."

The town council voted 9-4 last night to reduce the size of the town hall staff from 20 to 16 people, but left the details to the mayor, who was not present at the meeting because he was out of town at a state conference.

Contacted by phone this morning, Washington said he was "appalled" by the council's decision and would attempt to get it reversed.

9. AVOID GETTING TANGLED UP IN INTERNAL POLITICS OR IN-JOKES OR COMMENTS THAT ARE ONLY IMPORTANT TO THOSE WHO WERE PRESENT AT THE EVENT

People who attend regular meetings develop a certain camaraderie and common frame of reference. Suppose that one council member frequently asks for the water pitcher to be passed his way, and he gets teased about this at meeting after meeting. One evening, his colleagues surprise him by bringing in a special water pitcher with his name engraved on it, and they make a big deal out of presenting this to him with mock formality. This may be very amusing to people who always attend the meetings, including the regular reporters, but does it affect the public at large?

If not, leave it out.

Similarly, decisions about purely procedural things may be of interest only to those present. If a parliamentarian rules that amendments must be considered in a certain order before the main motion can be considered, that affects the way the meeting is conducted but not the ultimate effect on the general public.

10. INCLUDE ENOUGH BACKGROUND SO THAT THOSE NOT FAMILIAR WITH THE ISSUES CAN UNDERSTAND WHAT HAPPENED AND ITS SIGNIFICANCE

The question of how much background to include is a tricky one. On the one hand, it is wrong to assume that everyone reading the story has read all the previous stories. On the other hand, it is wrong to repeat everything in such detail that it will bore people familiar with the subject. Somewhere in the middle is a happy medium.

Remember that people move in and out of town all the time, and someone who is new to the area may read your story. Therefore, it is probably a good idea to mention the schools covered by the regional school district or to explain what areas are covered by a public water and sewer system.

Sometimes a short phrase can sum up a situation well enough to put the most recent development in perspective. For example, "Jones, who has been the subject of a two-year investigation by the Securities and Exchange Commission . . ." or "Martin, who has been the subject of a massive federal manhunt since he escaped from the federal prison in Danbury six months ago. . . ."

When covering a speech by a well-known person, it helps to include some brief biographic information about the speaker. The more famous the speaker, the less biographic information is necessary. If the talk is by a first-time candidate for public office, people will want to know the person's background. But if the talk is by the president of the United States or a United States senator, it is safe to assume that most people already know who the person is.

11. DO YOUR HOMEWORK BEFORE THE SPEECH OR MEETING

A reporter always should find out as much as possible about an event before covering it. If you are covering a speech, read biographic information about the speaker. If the speaker has published a book recently, read the book, or at least skim it and read reviews. Read news accounts of previous speeches by the same person. In some cases it may even be possible to obtain an advance copy of the speech.

If you are covering a meeting, ask for the agenda of the meeting and the minutes of previous meetings. Get a list of the important players at the meeting. Often elected boards have an executive secretary or staff person who does the bulk of the clerical work, and it is a good idea to meet that person and ask for a preview of what is likely to come up at the meeting.

12. DON'T BE AFRAID TO ASK QUESTIONS

It is a reporter's job to ask questions. Never hesitate to ask a question out of fear that it is a "dumb question." Even if it is, it is better to appear dumb when you ask the question than to appear dumb when you publish the story in a newspaper or it appears on a radio or television broadcast.

If you question a speaker after the speech is over and include the answers in your story, make it clear in the story what was said in the main talk and what was said in response to a question. Otherwise, people who heard the talk will say, "I was there, and I didn't hear the speaker say that."

13. DO NOT BECOME AN ACTIVE PARTICIPANT IN THE MEETING OR A DISTRACTION AT THE SPEECH

Although asking questions is important, do not interrupt the speech or meeting with them. A reporter should be an objective bystander and not affect the course of the event.

Some governmental boards have a specific time for questions from members of the press, but more often reporters have to approach members of the board after the meeting has adjourned. It is never a good idea to interrupt a meeting with a question because that makes the reporter a part of the process rather than an objective observer.

14. WRITE THE STORY AS SOON AS POSSIBLE

Even if the deadline is not pressing, it helps tremendously to write the story immediately after the meeting, whenever possible. It is impossible to write down everything that happens at a meeting or everything that is said at a speech or news conference. A reporter who is paying attention will retain a lot in short-term memory, and writing the story as soon as possible gets the information down on paper more accurately.

15. WHEN POSSIBLE, WRITE AN ADVANCE AS WELL AS A FOLLOW STORY

In newsroom jargon, a story written before an event is called an *advance,* and a story written after the event is called a *follow.* It helps to write the advance story first because that requires doing exactly the kind of research that will make the follow story stronger. However, if someone else was assigned to write the advance, be sure that you have read it.

Although advances typically are shorter stories, they serve a vital function in a democracy because they empower ordinary citizens. People reading the advance story can decide whether they want to attend the speech or meeting and make their views known.

16. KNOW THE CHARACTERS INVOLVED AND THE SPELLING OF THE NAMES

Before attending a speech or meeting, make sure that you know the names, titles, and proper spelling of the main characters involved. It helps to learn the pronunciations too. If you are completely unfamiliar with the cast of characters, ask someone who knows them to fill you in. A little hint such as, "Mr. Wilson is the one with the beard," can be invaluable.

> When I was a young reporter working for the Evening Sentinel in Carlisle, Pa., I was assigned to cover a meeting of a nearby regional school committee. The committee was meeting at a school in a town I had never been to. After wandering around some rural roads, I was hopelessly lost, so I stopped in a general store and asked for directions. I told the man behind the counter I was looking for the school committee meeting and that I thought they met in a nearby school.
>
> "Oh yes," he assured me. "They meet there all right. It's just up the road about a mile on the left. They meet in the library. When you go into the school, turn left at the main office." He obviously was familiar with the meetings.
>
> "And the chairman of the committee, do you know if it is still Mr. Bucher?" I asked, pronouncing it "butcher."
>
> The man laughed at me. "Well, if you call him that, you won't get much of a story," he said. Around here we pronounce it 'boo-ker.'"

How to Cover the Police and Courts

1. ACCURACY IS IMPORTANT IN ANY NEWS STORY, BUT IT TAKES ON ADDED IMPORTANCE WHEN COVERING POLICE AND COURT STORIES

News stories involving police and court actions are among the most important and sensitive stories that appear in the news media. Despite the importance of these stories, they are often assigned to inexperienced reporters. Accuracy is particularly important in such stories because a mistake in a story about criminal charges can easily damage someone's reputation, and that can lead to a libel suit.

Printing the wrong name or the wrong charge can do irreparable harm to people's reputations. So every fact and the spelling of every name must be double-checked in crime stories.

2. FIRST, MAKE SURE THAT YOU UNDERSTAND THE LEGAL SYSTEM YOU ARE COVERING

Reporters should not attempt to write police or crime stories without understanding the legal system. There are many good books on law for journalists, there are seminars and workshops for journalists on covering the law, and there are lawyers in your area who will be willing to discuss the issues and answer questions.

The following brief sketch only touches on the subject, and reporters covering legal issues should make more thorough studies of the legal system in their areas.

First of all, reporters must understand the difference between the two types of court cases, civil and criminal. In civil cases, one individual brings a lawsuit against another individual. In criminal cases, the state (or government) presses charges against a person for breaking a law. The two types of cases are handled entirely differently.

Within the world of criminal cases, there are serious crimes, known as *felonies*, and less serious crimes, known as *misdemeanors;* these are handled differently. Reporters also should familiarize themselves with the steps involved in bringing a person to justice. Sometimes the first step is for a warrant to be issued for a person's arrest. Then the person may be arrested. Remember, though, that *arrest* is really just a word for *stop.* Any time a police officer stops someone, that person is *arrested*. Later, the person may be *booked* and fingerprinted. The *arraignment* is when formal charges are filed, and a judge agrees that there is enough evidence to hold the suspect.

In serious cases, the prosecutors may decide to seek an *indictment* by a grand jury. This means that the evidence is presented before a group of citizens who are asked to decide whether or not there is enough evidence for the case to go to trial. Grand jury deliberations are secret, although the final decisions are public. The grand jury does not decide guilt or innocence.

If a case does go to trial, it may be heard by a judge or, in some cases, by a jury. This is another group of citizens, separate from a grand jury, and they do decide guilt or innocence.

Note that the *Associated Press Stylebook* says to, "Use *innocent*, rather than *not guilty*, in describing a defendant's plea or a jury's verdict, to guard against the word *not* being dropped inadvertently." Most, but not all, newspapers follow this policy.

3. REMEMBER THAT PEOPLE ARE INNOCENT UNTIL PROVEN GUILTY

Reporters should be very careful to report exactly what has occurred in a criminal situation and to never leap to conclusions. A person who has been arrested and charged with murder is not necessarily a murderer. Even if the reporter witnessed one person shoot another to death, the shooter is not a *murderer* until a judge and a jury convicts the person of murder. It is always possible that the jury will decide that the suspect acted in self-defense or that it was justifiable homicide. Not all killings are murder, so it is important to use the legal terms carefully.

If the police tell you that the suspect was caught with his hands in the cash drawer, it is important to attribute that information to the police. "Officer Mary Wilkinson said Smith was caught with his hands in the cash drawer," or "According to the police report, Smith was caught with his hands in the cash drawer." Even if it turns out later that Smith didn't do it, those statements are all safe in case of a libel suit if they are accurate accounts of what the police reported. However, to state flatly that "Smith was caught with his hands in the cash drawer" could place the reporter on the losing end of a libel suit if it turned out to be inaccurate later. See Chapter 33 for more information about libel and other legal issues.

4. BUILDING A GOOD RELATIONSHIP WITH LAW-ENFORCEMENT PERSONNEL IS VITAL TO BEING A GOOD POLICE REPORTER

A police reporter must work cooperatively with the police, and this requires a relationship of mutual trust and respect. Police are required to make certain minimal information public, but that bare minimum is not enough to make for good news stories. A good police reporter builds good relationships with the police so that the police are willing to provide additional information that makes the stories interesting. This doesn't happen overnight. It takes months of building friendships and building trust before a police officer will want to help a reporter by adding the interesting sidelights that make a story interesting. Good reporters get in the habit of stopping by the police station and getting to know the officers personally. Casual conversations about weather, families, sports, and local issues can break down barriers. Eventually, the reporter and the officer realize that they can help each other by cooperating.

5. TREAT POLICE OFFICERS AS YOU WOULD WANT TO BE TREATED—WITH RESPECT

The best way for reporters to build a good relationship with police officers is to treat them with respect. It may be irritating if a reporter wants information and the police officer does not want to divulge the information, but complaining about it doesn't help. Acknowledging the officers' situations and the difficulty of their jobs will help.

6. REMEMBER THAT POLICE OFFICERS HAVE THEIR JOBS TO DO AND REPORTERS HAVE THEIR JOBS TO DO

The job of the police is to protect the public. The job of the journalist is to inform the public. These are two different jobs. If, for example, there have been a series of rapes in an area, the police may want to keep that information secret so that they can catch the rapist without letting him know they are aware of his pattern. A reporter may believe that it is more important to let the public know that there is a rapist in the area.

There may be times when the police are investigating a crime and they want to keep some facts about the crime out of the press so that they can use them as part of their investigation, but reporters want to provide the public with all the information possible. There is no simple answer to this conflict.

7. A REPORTER MUST REMAIN AN OBJECTIVE OBSERVER AND NEVER ACT AS AN AGENT OF THE POLICE

Journalists should report the news, not make it. Reporters may gather information about a crime, but the purpose always should be to report the facts in news stories, not to do the job of the police. As soon as reporters become agents of the police department, they lose some of their credibility.

Ideally, the police should respect the job done by reporters, and vice versa. Occasionally, law-enforcement officials will ask a reporter to turn over notes, recordings, or photographs for use of the police or prosecutors. Most journalists resist these efforts on the grounds that they interfere with the independence of the press, which is protected by the First Amendment to the Constitution. This is a complex legal issue that has been the subject of numerous court cases.

Occasionally, members of the public will ask journalists to investigate suspected criminal activity. Although this is certainly part of an investigative reporter's role, most responsible journalists also will suggest that the caller contact the appropriate law-enforcement agency to make it clear that the police and the media play separate roles.

8. ALWAYS REPORT THE FINAL DISPOSITION OF CASES

A common complaint against the mass media is that arrests are reported more prominently than acquittals. Sometimes this does happen because the mix of available news is different every day. Perhaps when the mayor was charged with shoplifting, it may have been the biggest story of the day, so it was a headline on page one. A year later, when he was found not guilty by a jury, there may have been a forest fire threatening the town, and the mayor's story got relegated to an inside page. Or even worse, the lawyers involved may have reached an out-of-court agreement in which they agreed to drop the charges in exchange for some undisclosed settlement. It is hard to turn such sketchy information into an interesting news story.

Fairness demands, however, that responsible journalists tell the whole story or at least as much of it as possible. If a person is accused of a crime and later exonerated, that should be reported fully. When possible, the exoneration should be given as much prominence as the accusation.

One responsible way to handle this issue in newspapers is to decide which courts the newspaper will cover and make it a routine matter to ask the clerk of the court for all the arraignments and all the dispositions. These can be printed in a daily listing. Such listings are often very popular with readers. (This is not practical, of course, in radio or television news operations. Internet sites can include such listings, and some courts are posting them on their own Web sites.)

9. IN COVERING ACCIDENTS, LOOK FOR CAUSES AND THE USE OF SAFETY EQUIPMENT SUCH AS SEAT BELTS

One of the most common types of police news is the automobile accident. Why do the news media cover car crashes? Some attribute it to pure sensationalism. There is a derisive expression, "If it bleeds, it leads." It is true that people seem to have a fascination with situations in which people are injured or killed. Perhaps it relates to the universal fear of death. But most journalists believe that covering automobile accidents provides a public service. If people know more about the causes of such accidents, they can act in a way to better avoid them in the future. By covering accidents, the media can highlight dangerous situations and motivate people to drive more carefully.

This altruistic motivation is only served, however, if the news reports inform the public about the causes and contributing factors involved in accidents. For example, reporting that the same intersection has been the site of numerous accidents could help the community to decide to make safety improvements there. And reporting whether the victims were wearing seat belts could help people to make informed decisions about whether to use them or not. Such information also can raise the level of debate when legislatures are deciding whether to require seat belt use.

10. AVOID USING THE JARGON USED BY EMERGENCY PERSONNEL

All professions develop specialized vocabularies that are not shared by the general public. Such jargon should not be used in the mass media. If a police officer tells you they are "interrogating a John Doe with an MO matching the perp of a string of b&e's," that needs to be translated into everyday language. Perhaps the police are questioning an unidentified suspect in connection with a recent series of break-ins.

When the rescue squad tells you, "one white female was transported for treatment of lacerations and contusions and a fracture of the tibia," that also needs to be simplified. Perhaps a woman was taken to the hospital for treatment of a broken leg, cuts, and bruises.

Rescue personnel tend to use the word *transported* whenever people are taken to a hospital, but this is not the way most people talk. In news stories, reserve *transported* for people who end up with Kirk and Spock on the starship *Enterprise*.

11. AVOID USING THE WORD ALLEGEDLY

Bad police reporting has the words *alleged* and *allegedly* scattered through it. Apparently, some reporters are still laboring under the misconception that tossing in *allegedly* will protect them from a libel suit. It will not.

If you read that a woman is an "alleged prostitute" or a man is an "alleged mobster," what do you think? If you are like most reasonable people, you will think that she is a prostitute and he is a mobster. If they were able to prove that those statements are false and defamatory, they could win libel suits, no matter how many times the reporter wrote *alleged*.

What would have protected the reporter from a libel suit (and also would have better informed the public) would be to tell the readers who is doing the alleging. If the news story says—accurately—that the woman was charged by police with prostitution or that District Attorney Martha Mason in her opening statement referred to the man as a mobster, then the same folks could not win their libel suits. Even if they were found not guilty of the charges, journalists are legally protected when they accurately report the official statements of law-enforcement personnel. Giving the source of the allegation also has the added advantage of letting the readers decide whether they choose to believe the allegation, depending on whether they believe the police or the district attorney.

How to Cover Disasters and Tragedies

1. IN EMERGENCIES, REMEMBER THE BASICS: WHO, WHAT, WHERE, WHEN, WHY, AND HOW

All reporters, at some point in their careers, will be called on to cover some sort of disaster or tragedy. Such events come unexpectedly, giving you no time for preparation or research. What may be the biggest story of your career could be the one for which you are least prepared.

If an airliner crashes in the area you cover, a tornado, fire, or flood destroys part of your town, or terrorist attack occurs, you have to move quickly and write quickly. This is when it helps to remember the basics. Simply make sure that you get the answers to the "five W's": who, what, where, when, and why, plus how. It is also a good idea to stick with a simple, straightforward inverted-pyramid structure, listing facts in descending order of importance (see Chapter 15).

2. THERE IS NO SUBSTITUTE FOR BEING ON THE SCENE

Although it may be easier to reach officials by telephone from your desk in the newsroom, it is usually important to go to the scene of the disaster. You are the eyes and ears of your readers. They want to know what it looks like, sounds like, and smells like. They also want to know what it feels like to be there.

A vivid description of the scene using concrete nouns and verbs can provide needed information about what happened. For example, if a house has burned, describing the soot-stained teddy bear on the front porch may be a telling detail.

3. KEEP IN TOUCH WITH YOUR NEWSROOM

While you are gathering details at the scene, your editor or supervisor may be back in the newsroom wondering whether or not you are getting the story. During disasters, it is more important than ever to stay in touch with the newsroom. In major disasters, most organizations will assign as many reporters as possible to the story, so their work has to be coordinated. Keeping in close touch with the editor facilitates this coordination. This is no time for lone wolves or prima donnas.

4. GET WHAT YOU CAN AT THE SCENE, AND THEN RETURN TO THE OFFICE TO "WORK THE PHONES"

Every disaster is different, of course, but the general idea is to head to the scene of the tragedy to get whatever sights, sounds, and firsthand accounts you can and then to return to the newsroom to "work the phones." This means calling officials who can give you information for the story. Generally, this also includes the police, firefighters, emergency-management officials, and hospital personnel. Having been at the scene, you will have a better idea of what questions to ask. For example, you might be able to say, "I saw five people being placed in ambulances, Chief. Can you tell me what hospitals they went to?"

Remember that during a major disaster, emergency personnel will be overworked and extremely busy, so you cannot waste their time. Make it clear that you understand how busy they are, but that the public will want to know the situation, and you want to provide as much accurate information as possible.

5. LOOK FOR THE HUMAN ELEMENT

Whether at the scene or on the phone, always keep in mind that people are interested in other people. After the World Trade Center tragedy of Sept. 11, 2001, *The New York Times* won universal praise for their series of short personality profiles of the victims of the disaster. It was those stories, rather than accounts of the physical or monetary damage, that people remember.

In a situation where many people die, you do need to ask for an estimate of the overall death toll, but that number is likely to change in such situations. What will not change are the human stories of individual people who lost their lives or people who worked to rescue others or people who lost loved ones. Telling those stories can help heal a community in times of crisis.

6. PUT THE EVENT IN PERSPECTIVE

When disaster strikes, people are likely to want to know, "How bad is this?" Of course, any loss of life is tragic, but people want to know if a given airliner crash, for example, is the worst in history or the worst in recent memory. They may wonder if that particular airline has had other crashes or if that model plane has had problems.

In February of 2003, when 100 people died in a fire at The Station nightclub in Rhode Island, it was the most tragic fire in recent memory. Had there ever been a worse nightclub fire? The better news accounts mentioned that the worst nightclub fire in American history was at the Cocoanut Grove nightclub in Boston in 1942, when 492 people perished. This fact does not diminish the tragedy for those involved, but the Cocoanut Grove information puts the fire in historical perspective.

7. DON'T MAKE A BAD SITUATION WORSE

Reporters can serve a vital function in times of crisis, but irresponsible or thoughtless journalists can make things worse. Doing so hurts the community at large and also hurts the image and credibility of the mass media.

Interrupting emergency personnel when they are trying to save lives or perform important duties is never a good idea. Try to get the information from another source or at another time. Reporters also should be careful about the locations of their vehicles. Of course, you want to get as close as possible to the news event, but leaving your car where it creates a traffic hazard and might cause an accident is a bad idea. When interviewing people, reporters should show appropriate sensitivity. The classic negative image of a reporter thrusting a microphone in the face of a grieving survivor who just lost a loved one and asking, "How do you feel," serves no purpose other than making people hate the media.

Later, when writing their news stories, reporters need to be aware of potential damage that can be caused by their stories. When a tragedy or disaster occurs, people will want accurate information. There is no need to make the situation appear any worse than it really is. Exaggerating the damage or sensationalizing the situation just makes a bad situation worse.

8. COOPERATE WITH EMERGENCY PERSONNEL

Reporters have a vital role to play during disasters, and so do the police, firefighters, and EMTs. Occasionally, these jobs conflict. Sometimes emergency officials will make special accommodations for members of the media, so it doesn't hurt to make sure that they know you are a working reporter. If they still insist that you leave, do what they say.

If an officer tells you to get out of the way or to leave an area, that is not a good time to get into a philosophical discussion of the importance of the First Amendment. It is usually a better idea to comply with the orders at the time and later discuss the situation with a superior officer to ensure better access next time.

9. TALK TO ORDINARY PEOPLE AFFECTED BY THE EVENTS

When a disaster strikes, reporters are trained to go straight to the official sources, such as the police chief, the fire chief, or the nursing supervisor at the hospital. Those sources are important, but it also helps to talk to the ordinary people who may be directly affected by the incident.

The police chief may be able to tell you that 60 families were evacuated when the river flooded, but the real human story will come from the people who had to leave their homes. The Coast Guard officer can tell you about the rescue operation, but the fisherman who was plucked off the deck of his sinking vessel will have the unforgettable story.

10. DON'T BE AFRAID TO EXPRESS YOUR CONDOLENCES TO PEOPLE WHO HAVE LOST LOVED ONES

Occasionally, an editor will assign a reporter to interview someone who has lost a loved one. It is never an easy assignment, but if you handle it with sensitivity and compassion, it can go well. Start by expressing sympathy. People appreciate expressions of compassion. Grieving relatives also may have a genuine desire to talk about their loved one, but if they do not, don't push it. You might ask if there is someone willing to speak for the family. You might point out that your readers, listeners, or viewers will want to know about the person who died and that you would like to tell them about your source's relative. Chances are that the relatives may like the idea of letting people know what a good person their loved one was.

11. GIVE PEOPLE AN OPPORTUNITY TO TALK IF THEY WANT TO

If a relative feels like talking, just let him or her tell the story his or her own way. Some of their stories may not be usable, but don't be rude. When dealing with a grieving relative, the best approach is to let him or her talk and respond sympathetically. If you can gently guide the person toward specific examples and usable anecdotes, this is good, but sometimes you just have to let the person pour out his or her heart.

12. LOOK FOR THE STORIES OTHERS MAY HAVE MISSED

In major disasters or tragedies, there are likely to be many journalists covering the story. In such a case, try looking around for the less obvious story behind the story. If hundreds of reporters are standing at a news conference, all looking at the speaker in front, try looking in the other direction, both literally and figuratively. All the other reporters will get the main story of the big announcement by the public official. Is there another story going on elsewhere?

Perhaps the drivers who brought the speakers to the scene have some interesting comments or observations. Perhaps the security arrangements around the perimeter of the site would make a good sidebar story. Will the media frenzy affect the budget of the local police department? How do the local reporters feel about having their territory invaded by the national press corps?

There are plenty of stories surrounding the one big story, and some of them might be more interesting than the obvious one. All it takes is the flexibility to look in the less obvious places.

On March 28, 1979, I was driving on Interstate 81 near my home in Carlisle, Pa., when the radio said there had been an accident at the nearby Three Mile Island Nuclear Power Plant. I was a staff reporter for the *Evening Sentinel* in Carlisle. Copy Editor Rick Wakely was with me. We decided to swing by "TMI" to see what was going on. I stopped a worker coming out of the plant, and he told me there had been a partial meltdown that damaged about half of the core, and a small amount of radiation was released into the atmosphere.

We reported that information in the next day's edition of the *Evening Sentinel,* although the owners of the plant denied it later. Eventually an investigation by the Nuclear Regulatory Commission confirmed what the worker told me.

By the second day of the crisis, hundreds of reporters from all over the world descended on Middletown, Pa., which was on the edge of our coverage area. A makeshift media center was set up in a recreation center, and the telephone company sold lines to the various media. I had one of a hundred phones set up on folding tables in the gym.

One day I looked at the reporter next to me and was about to complain about his cigar. But I recognized him as Jimmy Breslin, the world-famous columnist for the *New York Daily News.* Breslin (who went on to win a Pulitzer Prize for commentary in 1986) was a folk hero among journalists. I stammered an introduction and asked him if he could offer any advice to a young reporter.

"Hoofin' it!" he bellowed. "Get out there and hit the streets. There's no damn news in here," he said, waving his cigar-laden hand toward the gymnasium filled with scores of journalists.

"The stories are all out there. Talk to real people—not these flacks."

The "flacks" were public relations specialists for the state, the NRC, the utility company that owned the plant and other official agencies. They gave regular briefings in the gym.

I took Breslin's advice and walked around the neighborhood near the plant and discovered, to my surprise, that the closest neighbors were all big supporters of the plant. The neighbors didn't want the plant shut down; they said it was a good neighbor that had brought economic prosperity and clean energy to the neighborhood. I got a great story by 'hoofin' it.

How to Write Obituaries

1. ACCURACY IS ESPECIALLY IMPORTANT IN OBITUARIES

Of course, accuracy is important in any story, but it takes on special importance in obituaries. There are three main reasons for this: Obituaries are well read; they are clipped out as mementoes; and they are the only time many people get mentioned in the newspaper.

Readership studies show that obituaries are among the best-read sections of any newspaper. Thus, if there is a mistake in an obituary, lots of people will see it.

Obituaries are more than news stories; they are important family records. Many people cut out copies of obituaries and save them. Therefore, a mistake in an obituary is particularly upsetting. Even if a correction appears later, that does not give the bereaved relative a clipping to save. For this reason, many newspapers agree to completely reprint an obituary with the corrections.

Sad as it may sound, an obituary is the only time most people are mentioned in a newspaper. The deceased person will never know if there was a mistake, but all the friends and relatives of the deceased will know about it and discuss it at the funeral. This is enough to ruin the reputation of a newspaper.

2. LEARN YOUR PUBLICATION'S POLICIES ABOUT OBITUARIES

Different newspapers have different policies about obituaries. Small local papers tend to print every obituary sent their way. Larger metropolitan newspapers usually select only the most newsworthy obituaries. Some newspapers require a cause of death, whereas others do not pursue that information. Some newspapers edit obituaries more than others. Some newspapers treat obituaries as advertisements, allowing families to write whatever they like if they pay the fee. Many newspapers provide electronic guest books on their Web sites.

3. UNDERSTAND THE DIFFERENCE BETWEEN A NEWS OBITUARY AND A PAID FUNERAL NOTICE

Although policies vary, most newspapers print two kinds of information about deaths. One is an advertisement; the other is a news story.

The first, called a *death notice, funeral notice,* or *paid obit,* is an advertisement written by funeral directors and paid for by the family through the funeral home. Death notices usually are handled by a newspaper's classified advertising department, and the wording is completely up to the person paying the bill.

The second type of information is a news story, usually called an *obituary* or *news obit.* The obituary is basically a news story, so it should be clear, concise, and accurate. It should follow the style of news stories and provide all the important information. It should include enough information about the deceased so that people know why that person was important. Unlike a paid funeral notice, the wording of a news obituary is not dictated by the funeral home.

Typically, newspapers receive information about deaths from funeral directors, who are not trained journalists. They may not include all the information a reporter needs to know. That is when the reporter should call friends and family members to get more information about the person who died.

Most newspapers are willing to accept obituary information from members of the family, without going through a funeral director.

4. UNDERSTAND THE ROLE OF FUNERAL DIRECTORS IN OBITUARIES

Funeral directors sell their services to the families of the deceased, and usually they include a charge for placing obituaries. In exchange for a fee, the funeral director will interview the person making funeral arrangements and provide the bare facts of the person's life, including survivors and occupation. The funeral director typically will pay for a funeral notice advertisement and also request a news obituary with the same information.

A good funeral director will work cooperatively with the local newspapers and help to promote accuracy. Frequently, a funeral director will help a reporter get in touch with a family member who is willing to act as a representative for the family and talk to the press about the deceased.

5. REMEMBER THAT YOU ARE PROFILING A PERSON'S LIFE, NOT JUST COVERING A DEATH

Although a basic obituary may only say that a person died and list a few jobs and survivors, a good obituary tells about the person's life. Everyone has a story, and that story is interesting to most people. A good obituary writer will make the effort to find out the story behind every person. For example, a funeral director may mention that the deceased was a U.S. Army veteran. A reporter could ask about the nature of the person's army service and discover that the person was a part of the dramatic Berlin Airlift that brought supplies to the residents of West Berlin during the Russian blockade in 1948 and 1949.

6. EVERYONE HAS A STORY

The stories are there; the hard part is finding them. If a reporter makes the effort to ask, it is very likely that a relative will want to talk about his or her loved one. The reporter should ask for specific anecdotes and stories. If the person says that her grandmother enjoyed cooking, ask for a specific dish for which the grandmother was particularly known.

7. DO NOT HESITATE TO CONTACT THE NEXT OF KIN

At first, it seems rude and insensitive to call the next of kin of a person who has died, but people want to see an obituary that is accurate and complete. So call the home and ask if someone would be willing to talk about the person whose obituary you are preparing. You might say something like, "I am very sorry about your loss, and I know this is a difficult time, but we would like our readers to know a little about your brother."

8. PEOPLE WILL WANT TO KNOW THE CAUSE OF DEATH

Funeral directors traditionally use euphemisms such as "died suddenly," "died unexpect-edly," or "died after a short illness." For many years these phrases were used to disguise the cause of death because stigmas were associated with various illnesses. But the euphemisms have outlived the stigmas. Now most families will be perfectly happy to provide the cause of death. After all, when someone dies, that is one of the first questions people ask.

When I started working at the Cape Cod Times, I met a freelance writer named Craig Little. He was a delightful fellow with a vast storehouse of jokes, anecdotes, and stories that made him very popular in the newsroom and at parties. He was also a very prolific writer. Craig could knock out a good story in a few hours. That made him very popular with editors, who suddenly found they had more pages to fill than they had stories.

Then Craig got tired of the uncertainties of freelance writing and took a regular salaried position as an editor of a medical journal in the New York area. After about 10 years, I ran into him on Cape Cod again. He had moved back to the Cape with his wife, who was from Switzerland. I saw them at a party once and complimented Craig on how much weight he had lost. I told him he looked great. I had no idea he was dying of cancer.

When Craig died, a young reporter at the *Times* was assigned to write his obituary. Craig's children have French names, and the obituary writer, Sean, got them wrong. I had been mentoring Sean and encouraging him for a few years, but this time I let him have it. I was about to go to the funeral and talk to Craig's widow. How was I going to explain to her how Craig's old newspaper couldn't even get the spelling of their children's names right? What the hell was he thinking?

"Why are you yelling at me?" Sean asked. "You know I am a good reporter and I get everything right 90 percent of the time."

Well, 90 percent accuracy isn't good enough when you are writing an obituary. Reporters may only get chewed out if the inaccuracies occur in the obituary of their editor's old friend, but someone is going to be very upset by any mistake in any obituary.

How to Write Reviews and Criticism

Most newspapers and magazines and many television and radio stations include reviews of books, plays, films, concerts, and recordings. There are many Web sites devoted to reviews and criticism. The purpose of the reviews is to inform the public about what is available and to help people decide whether they want to see a show, attend a performance, or buy a book or recording.

Some people draw a distinction between a reviewer and a critic. The word *critic* is used to describe a writer who has demonstrated expertise in a field and therefore can write with greater authority on that subject. A *reviewer,* in contrast, can be anyone who wants to review a performance. Not everyone draws that distinction, and for the most part, the rules are the same.

1. DO YOUR HOMEWORK BEFORE THE SHOW. FIND OUT AS MUCH BACKGROUND INFORMATION AS POSSIBLE

If you are assigned to review a performance, learn as much as possible before the performance. Many plays and films are based on books, and it is always a good idea to read the book first, if possible. This will give you a common frame of reference with others who have read the book. Telling people whether the film is faithful to the book is a useful piece of information. The reviewer should at least be familiar with the subject.

2. COME PREPARED. BE SURE TO HAVE A NOTEBOOK AND PEN OR PENCIL. TAKE NOTES SPARINGLY. JUST NOTE A FEW KEY ITEMS TO REMEMBER

Sitting in the audience watching a play, a performance, or a film is not a good time to be writing constantly. Sit back and enjoy the show. There will be a few times when you will want to make note of special things to mention in your review. Write down enough detail to remind yourself what you were thinking without writing out the whole paragraph. You will want to have a notebook and pen, plus a small penlight flashlight.

3. ARRIVE EARLY AND STAY LATE. IT'S NOT FAIR TO WRITE A REVIEW OF A PERFORMANCE IF YOU MISSED PART OF IT. BE SURE TO READ ALL THE CREDITS AT THE END OF A FILM

A reviewer takes on the responsibility of letting a larger audience know about the show. It would be irresponsible to present an evaluation of a show without seeing the whole thing.

Another reason to arrive early and stay late is the chance to pick up little tidbits. Before a play begins, for example, the director may announce a change in cast that does not appear in the program. Another example is the credits at the end of a film. The "special thanks" or production notes may include a local reference or interesting note that would interest the readers of the review. In any case, missing such notes will hurt the review.

4. PAY ATTENTION TO THE AUDIENCE'S REACTION. NOTE HOW MANY PEOPLE ATTENDED, AND TRY TO JUDGE THEIR REACTIONS

Describing the audience's reaction will help readers to decide whether they are likely to enjoy the performance. If an enthusiastic full house was on its feet, clapping and cheering, that says one thing. If the show was attended sparsely and many folks left in the middle, that says something else. Did people laugh at the jokes or sing along with the songs? All that can be part of a review. In the case of a book, the equivalent would be to mention whether the book is selling well.

5. WRITE YOUR REVIEW AS SOON AS POSSIBLE AFTER THE PERFORMANCE. "STRIKE WHILE THE IRON IS HOT"

Your first reaction is usually the most valid. If your deadline allows it, you may want to revise the review later, but a first draft should be written immediately after the performance. Back in the days when blacksmiths fabricated tools out of iron, they would hold the iron in a fire and then strike it with a hammer while it was still hot enough to be molded. The principle has many applications beyond the blacksmith's craft. Since a reporter cannot write down everything about a performance, much of the review will come from memory, and memory is sharpest immediately after a performance. It is best to write the review as soon as possible after the performance.

6. MAKE IT PERFECTLY CLEAR IN THE LEAD WHAT YOUR MAIN POINT IS. CHOOSE ONE MAIN THEME AND STICK TO IT

Like any good piece of news writing, a review can make only one main point. Decide that first, and make that point in the first sentence or two. Do not leave the reader guessing about whether you liked the show or not.

For example, your point could be that the play was poor because of a weak performance by the lead actor:

A tone-deaf "Music Man" spoiled the opening production by the Suburban Theater Company last night.

Or your point could be that the film was excellent:

The quirky charm of Kevin Spacey and Judi Dench bring "The Shipping News" to life in the fine film version of Annie Proulx's Pulitzer Prize–winning novel.

7. BE SURE TO IDENTIFY THE MAJOR CHARACTERS AND ACTORS OR PERFORMERS SO THAT THE READERS WILL RECOGNIZE THEM FROM OTHER PERFORMANCES, WHERE APPROPRIATE

When reviewing films or plays, it helps to identify the actors in terms the audience will understand. For example:

"Holy Smoke" stars Kate Winslet, who gained fame as one of the star-crossed lovers in "Titanic."

In a concert, you might want to make note of the performers, such as

Paul McCartney was backed up by guitarist Robbie McIntosh, former lead guitarist in The Pretenders.

Do not assume that your readers are familiar with the same performers you are.

8. INCLUDE A BRIEF PLOT SUMMARY, BUT DO NOT DEVOTE YOUR ENTIRE REVIEW TO IT

The readers will want a little information about the plot of a book, play, or film but not too much. It is certainly a mistake to give away a surprise ending or to bore readers with too much detail. A general idea of the subject matter is usually sufficient. Ask yourself if the readers will need to know all those details to decide whether they want to see the show or read the book.

9. GIVE READERS ENOUGH INFORMATION TO LET THEM KNOW WHETHER THEY WANT TO SEE IT THEMSELVES

Readers need to know the nuts and bolts of the performance to help them decide whether to attend. This includes, of course, the date, time, place, and price, as well as the availability of tickets. It also includes the ratings of films and similar information about a play or other performance. Readers will want to know if it includes sex, nudity, violence, and/or profanity. This will help them to decide not only whether they want to attend themselves but also whether they want to bring their children.

It is not always necessary to make a value judgment about such aspects. Just providing the information will allow your readers to make up their own minds.

10. STATE YOUR OPINION CLEARLY AND USUALLY WITHOUT THE USE OF FIRST PERSON. THERE IS RARELY ANY NEED TO SAY, "I THINK," BECAUSE THE READER ASSUMES THAT THE OPINIONS ARE THOSE OF THE REVIEWER

Unlike most news writing, reviews do include the opinion of the writer. They should be marked clearly as a review so that readers will not be surprised by seeing opinions clearly stated. There is no need to qualify your opinions with phrases such as "I think" or "in this reviewer's opinion" because that is understood.

However, the best reviewers back up their opinions with examples and details. This makes the reader more likely to accept those opinions.

11. INCLUDE SPECIFIC DETAILS TO BACK UP YOUR OPINIONS. MENTION INDIVIDUAL PERFORMERS, CHARACTERS, AND SCENES

If you say a performance is disappointing, give examples to prove your point. "Juliette's voice was so weak that it did not carry to the middle of the theater" would give people a good idea of what to expect. Or "the band's renditions of their golden oldies had the audience literally dancing in the aisles."

Like any good reporting, reviewing is built on specific details with nouns and verbs, not casual, vague adjectives and adverbs.

12. HAVE FUN, RELAX, AND MAKE THE TONE OF THE REVIEW APPROPRIATE TO THE TONE OF THE PERFORMANCE

Tone is a difficult technique to describe, but it is important in reviews. A review of a performance by the alternative rock band Barenaked Ladies obviously will be more lighthearted than a review of a performance of *Hamlet*. A performance of a comedian should include a few examples of the jokes in the routine, but jokes normally have no place in a review of a performance of a classical string quartet.

This is another reason it is a good idea to write the review immediately after seeing the performance. The mood of the performance will affect the way you write.

13. ACCURACY IS AS IMPORTANT IN A REVIEW AS IN ANY OTHER PIECE OF JOURNALISM. SPELL THE PEOPLE'S NAMES RIGHT, AND GET THE DETAILS RIGHT

Mistakes can ruin a review, just as they can ruin any news story. If a reviewer misspells the name of a performer or lists an actor in the wrong part, it destroys the credibility of the review. People who notice the review will tend to dismiss the accuracy of everything else in the review. Even worse, they will be suspicious about everything else in the publication.

Once, in the 1990s, I volunteered to review a performance of folksingers Peter, Paul, and Mary at the Cape Cod Melody Tent in Hyannis, Mass. I had been to several of their concerts since the 1960s, so I pretty much knew what to expect. In fact, I even wrote some background material, known as "B-copy," in advance to save time, since the deadline was very soon after the performance was expected to end. But the performance ran long—much to everyone else's delight—and I was worried about missing my deadline. So I left early and headed to my car. But someone had parked directly behind my car, blocking me in. I had no choice but to go back and watch the end of the show. I got back to my seat just in time to hear Mary Travers talk about the thrill of having once performed "If I Had a Hammer" for President John F. Kennedy. She said she was talking about that experience earlier in the evening with President Kennedy's brother, Sen. Edward M. Kennedy, who was in the audience—and she introduced him. That incident made it unlike any other Peter, Paul, and Mary concert, and I would have missed it had I been able to leave early. I still got back to the newsroom in time to include that in my review.

How to Write Editorials and Columns

Several different kinds of opinion pieces can be found on the opinion pages of newspapers and magazines. They include editorials, opinion columns, political columns, personal columns, humor columns, and advice columns. These same categories appear in slightly different forms in radio, television, and the emerging digital media.

An *editorial* is an unsigned statement by the editorial board of a newspaper. Editorials are short, argumentative essays designed to show opinion leadership. They are designed to convince the readership of a point of view.

An *opinion column* is a journalistic essay expressing an opinion on a matter of public discourse. Newspapers and magazines generally print only those that have special merit because of the quality of the writing or the expertise of the writer. These are sometimes called *op/ed columns* because they frequently appear on the *op/ed page,* which is the page opposite the editorial page.

A *political column* is an opinion column written by an expert in politics. Political columns are designed to argue a particular political point of view. The best political columns include evidence and research to back up the opinions.

A *personal column* is a personal statement by a writer who brings his or her own experiences to the writing to make a point, to inform, or to entertain. Personal columns often use a first-person point of view.

A *humor column* is a special kind of personal column. Humor columns are designed to amuse and entertain readers with satire, sarcasm, puns, jokes, and other forms of humor. The best ones also comment on current political or social situations. Dave Barry, humor columnist for the *Miami Herald,* was known for his silly slapstick style of humor, yet he won a Pulitzer Prize for commentary in 1988.

An *advice column* offers advice to readers based on the writer's expertise. The best ones offer background and evidence to substantiate the advice. Many advice columns are in specialized areas, such as personal finance, automotive maintenance, travel, or cooking.

Most newspapers and magazines also publish *letters to the editor,* which are brief statements of opinion by members of the public.

The following rules apply most directly to the first three categories: editorials, opinion columns, and political columns.

As traditional newspapers embrace and converge with the new media, advice and opinion columns have become available in a variety of forms.

Between 2005 and 2007, *The New York Times* offered access to its most popular opinion columns (such as Thomas Friedman and Maureen Dowd) online only to subscribers paying $7.95 per month. It was offered free to regular home delivery subscribers. In the fall of 2007, the *Times* discontinued this program and made all its content available without charge.

1. DETERMINE YOUR GOAL. WHY ARE YOU WRITING THIS OPINION ARTICLE? WHAT IS YOUR MAIN POINT? WHAT DO YOU HOPE TO ACHIEVE?

Determining your specific goal is the most important step in writing any opinion piece. You may have a variety of opinions in any given area, but it is vital to limit yourself to one specific subject if you want to write a clear, coherent piece of writing. Remember, the goal of any opinion piece is to convince someone of something. If you are not clear about what it is you are trying to achieve, you are doomed to fail.

2. DETERMINE YOUR AUDIENCE. WHO ARE YOU TRYING TO CONVINCE? WHAT ARE THEIR ATTITUDES ON THE SUBJECT? HOW CAN YOU BEST BRING THEM TO AGREE WITH YOUR POINT OF VIEW?

Your audience will determine your approach. If, for example, you want to argue that marijuana should be legalized, you must determine whom it is you want to convince. If your audience is a group of young, liberal college students, you would take one approach, but if your audience is members of a conservative state legislature, you would take another approach. If you are writing to the general public, you might want to urge them to contact their legislators, but if you are writing to the legislators themselves, you could urge them to vote a certain way on a certain bill. Be certain that you have a clear idea of your audience, and address them directly.

3. OUTLINE YOUR ARGUMENT. DESIGN A LOGICAL TRAIN OF THOUGHT THAT LEADS TO YOUR CONCLUSION

An outline is as important in opinion writing as in any other kind of writing. Make sure that you have a clear pattern of development, and stick with it. Start with areas of agreement and slowly build to your recommendation, bringing the reader along with you. It will help if the readers are saying to themselves, "Oh, yes, I see where the writer is going with this. That makes sense." Simplistic statements such as, "There are three reasons why this will work," can be extremely effective as organizational techniques.

4. BEGIN WITH A CATCHY LEAD THAT WILL GET PEOPLE TO READ YOUR ARTICLE. DO NOT TURN AWAY READERS WITH AN UNPOPULAR OPINION IN THE FIRST SENTENCE

The most powerful opinion piece is useless if nobody reads it, so make the lead interesting. If you know that your point is going to be unpopular, build up to it slowly. Arguing in favor of higher taxes is always a hard sell, but it is possible to get people to agree with you if you explain the benefits they will receive from the programs supported with those taxes.

5. START OUT WITH AREAS OF AGREEMENT. BEGIN WITH STATEMENTS ON WHICH MOST PEOPLE AGREE. BUILD FROM THERE WITH SIMPLE, LOGICAL STEPS

Everyone needs food, clothing, and shelter. Everyone can relate to those needs. Everyone wants to live in peace, harmony, and tranquility. People generally want their children to have a good life and safe environment. Most people are in favor of love, beauty, honesty, fair play, and the truth. People love Superman because he fights for "truth, justice, and the American way." Those are areas of agreement. If you start there and show how your proposal will support, uphold, or further one of those universal feelings, your opinion will be respected.

6. FOLLOW UNIVERSAL RULES OF LOGIC. USE "IF . . . THEN" ARGUMENTS AND OTHER GENERALLY ACCEPTED CONCEPTS

Readers will follow a clear, logical argument. They will not follow a disjointed argument that jumps from point to point without any clear pattern. Simple "if . . . then" statements work best. For example, you might say, "If dependence on foreign oil and air pollution are problems, and if the excessive use of private cars contributes to both these problems, then we should support public transportation." People still may disagree with you, but at least your argument would be easy to follow.

7. BUILD TOWARD THE PARTICULAR ACTION YOU ADVOCATE SO THAT THE READER COMES ALONG WITH YOU

First, state some general principles with which the readers will agree. Then demonstrate how your new proposal will go along with those general principles. Then ask your readers to take specific actions that will lead to implementation of your policy. In the public transportation example above, for example, you might want to urge a governmental body to adopt a transportation plan, urge members of the public to write to their representatives advocating such a plan, or even urge members of the public to give up their cars and try using the public transportation that is available.

8. NEVER OVERSTATE YOUR CASE. IF YOU GO TOO FAR, YOU WILL LOSE READERS

Once you have made your point, don't get carried away. If you have convinced readers that some public transportation can be beneficial, do not try to convince them to give up their cars entirely. Most people would find that unrealistic.

Similarly, you might argue that Americans should adopt a more healthful diet by eating more fruits and vegetables. To go on and argue that all fast-food restaurants should be outlawed, however, probably would not gain widespread support.

9. DON'T BE WISHY-WASHY. ONCE YOU HAVE BUILT UP YOUR CASE, STATE IT FIRMLY AND CLEARLY. DO NOT BACK AWAY FROM IT IN THE END

Having made your point, stick with it. Nothing weakens an editorial more than a weak ending that backs away from the position. If you have argued convincingly that the new recreation center is a good idea, don't back off at the last minute with a cop-out statement such as, "Even if it is not a good idea, we ought to go ahead with the plans."

10. FOLLOW ALL THE RULES OF GOOD WRITING, INCLUDING USE OF STRONG ACTION VERBS, SHORT SENTENCES, AND GOOD GRAMMAR

Clear, concise news writing is made up of strong, short sentences. Do not make the mistake of thinking that the editorial page is a haven for long, convoluted sentences. In general, the more complex the information, the shorter the sentences should be.

11. EDITORIALS ARE THE VOICE OF THE LEADERSHIP OF A NEWSPAPER

Editorials are a special kind of opinion writing. They are usually unsigned and rarely use the first person. Traditionally, any first-person references are in the "editorial we." Their purpose is to urge readers to follow a course of action advocated by the leadership of the newspaper. Most newspapers have an editorial board that includes the editor of the newspaper and others. Editorials may be written by a variety of people, but they are approved by the editorial board.

12. OPINION COLUMNS EXPRESS THE PERSONAL OPINION OF THE WRITER

Opinion columns, including political columns and personal columns, have a byline or "column sig" that identifies the writer. They usually include an identifying "tag line" that tells the reader something about the writer. Good newspapers endeavor to present a variety of opinion columns from various points of view.

Most columnists have "paid their dues" by working as news reporters or editors or in other fields before earning the right to publish their opinions. Unsubstantiated opinions with little to back them up are not popular with readers or editors.

You never know where an opinion column will lead.

Once I was asked to write one of a series of columns about various religious traditions. Mine was titled, "Why We Are Buddhists." It was fairly well received at the time it was published, and I gave it little thought after that. But five years later I met a man who recognized my name. "Are you the guy who wrote 'Why We Are Buddhists'?" he asked me. He said that the column changed his life because he was a teenager trying to explain to his parents what he believed spiritually. When he read the column, he gave it to them and said, "Here, read this. It is what I believe."

How to Write Feature Stories

1. FEATURE STORIES MUST HAVE SOMETHING TO GRAB AND HOLD READERS' INTEREST OTHER THAN THE NEWSWORTHINESS OF HARD NEWS STORIES

Although every news story is unique, journalists tend to group them into broad categories for simplicity. One way to divide stories is to classify them as either news or features. In newsroom slang, these are sometimes called "hard" or "soft" stories, respectively.

A hard news story tends to be a simple, straightforward report of a recent significant event. It is likely to use an inverted-pyramid structure (see Chapter 15) and few special writing techniques.

A soft feature story tends to use more creative writing techniques to heighten interest in a subject that might not be as inherently newsworthy. Feature stories may include a narrative storytelling style, a question-and-answer format, a humorous angle, or other techniques found in creative writing.

These categories are useful for analysis and story, but in the real world of news writing, stories come in many different shapes, sizes, and styles. It may be difficult to fit a specific story into a specific category.

2. TO FEATURE SOMETHING IS TO DRAW ATTENTION TO IT. A GOOD FEATURE STORY USES EXCEPTIONAL WRITING TO DRAW ATTENTION TO SOMETHING

The word *feature* has many meanings in the English language. It is used to mean a part of the human face or the main presentation at a movie theater. In most situations, a feature stands out for some reason. As a verb, *to feature* is to give something prominence or make it stand out. In news writing, a feature story is a story that stands out because of its writing.

3. FEATURE STORIES HEIGHTEN INTEREST WITH LITERARY TECHNIQUES SUCH AS IRONY, CONTRAST, DRAMA, SUSPENSE, AND DIALOGUE

Listing elements of effective feature writing is much easier than using them success-fully. It is much too simplistic to think that a reporter can just take a news event and toss in some irony, contrast, and drama and end up with a great feature. Using them effectively depends on understanding the techniques and applying them to appropri-ate situations.

Irony is perhaps the trickiest. Most dictionaries define *irony* as "the use of words to convey a meaning different from or opposite from their literal meaning." A related term, *dramatic irony,* is a literary technique in which the outcome of events is contrary to what might be expected.

Some people casually use it to mean any surprising coincidence, but that is stretching the meaning. A song by Alanis Morissette entitled "Ironic" lists some strange coincidences, such as an old man winning the lottery and dying the next day or rain occurring on your wedding day. Many are sad, but none of them is truly ironic, according to the strict definition.

When the musician Paul Simon was honored for his contributions to performing arts in America at the annual Kennedy Center Honors in 2002, writer, actor, and humorist Steve Martin was chosen to give the speech honoring Simon.

"It would be easy to stand here and talk about Paul Simon's intelligence and skill," said Martin, "but this is neither the time nor the place."

The audience laughed heartily at Martin's perfect sense of irony.

So how do you use irony in a feature story? There was a news story in the *Cape Cod Times* one year that stated that according to the FBI crime statistics, the tiny town of Truro, Mass., with a population of about 2,000 people, had the largest increase in murder rates in the state. The 100 percent increase topped every other town in the report, including Boston. Of course, the increase was from zero to one.

Contrast, drama, suspense, and dialogue are other literary devices common in feature stories. Whereas a straight news story includes occasional quotes from one or two sources, a feature story could report an entire conversation between two people in the form of dialogue.

4. FEATURE STORIES MUST ADHERE TO BASIC JOURNALISTIC PRINCIPLES; THEY MUST BE FACTUAL, FAIR, BALANCED, AND COMPLETE

Feature writers may get a "poetic license" to use unconventional writing techniques, but they get no license to violate the principles of good news writing. Make sure that all facts are accurate and that the finished story is balanced and fair. Unlike writers of fiction, the news writer is constrained by the limits of real life. So do not get carried away by your literary idea of a beautiful story. Maybe it would be sweet to make it look like everybody lived happily ever after, but if the facts don't support that story, you can't use it.

5. THE BEST FEATURE STORIES ARE BUILT ON NOUNS AND VERBS, WITH VERY FEW ADJECTIVES

Amateurs may think that feature writing is the time to drag out lots of adjectives and adverbs, but that is not the case. Good, strong nouns and verbs are the key to good feature writing, as they are the key to all good writing.

Instead of saying the man was tall, say that he was 6-feet, 6-inches tall, or say that he ducked his head as he went through the doorway. Instead of saying that the coffee was hot, say that as soon as the man let the coffee touch his lips, he spat it out sputtering and fanning his mouth.

6. A FEATURE STORY SHOULD BE BASED ON ONE SINGLE POINT, AND THAT SHOULD BE STATED IN A "NUT GRAF" NEAR THE BEGINNING

Feature stories may touch on many different aspects of a subject, but they should be based on one clear, concise point. You should be able to write that point down in one simple sentence of fewer than 25 words. Write that statement down before you write your feature story. Perhaps it should be the lead of your story. Perhaps it should be the "nut graf" that comes after a short feature lead. Perhaps it should appear in another form, but it should be there near the beginning of the story.

7. THE CHRONOLOGICAL STORYTELLING METHOD OF WRITING MAY BE APPROPRIATE FOR SOME FEATURE STORIES

People are all storytellers to one extent or another. Everyone loves a good story. Writers of feature stories can benefit from this natural human tendency by using the chronological storytelling technique. Before launching into the narrative, though, it is important to let the reader know why it is worth sticking with the story. You may have to foreshadow the ending or explain the significance of the story before launching into the chronology.

It could be as simple as saying something like,

It was an adventure Bill Richards and Mary Smith will never forget.

"If it hadn't been for the kindness of a passing stranger, we wouldn't be here to tell the story," said Smith.

It all began at 5 a.m. Tuesday when the New Rochelle, N.Y., couple set out for a long weekend in the White Mountains of New Hampshire . . .

8. GOOD FEATURE WRITING DEPENDS ON COLLECTING AND SELECTING SPECIFIC DETAILS THAT ILLUSTRATE THE POINT OF THE STORY

People put together big pictures by assembling a collection of details. This is the way the human mind works. If you can collect a series of details about one subject, eventually they will paint your picture for you. Photographs in newspapers are made up of thousands of tiny dots. It is the assemblage of those tiny details that create the big picture.

For example, simply stating that the woman appeared nervous may not convince the reader. If you explain that she looked over her shoulder several times during the interview, that her eyes darted around the room, and that she kept straightening out her skirt and smoothing her hair, it begins to present the portrait of a nervous woman.

9. FEATURE STORIES ARE SOMETIMES CALLED HUMAN INTEREST STORIES. THE BEST FEATURE STORIES STRESS THE HUMANITY THAT WE ALL SHARE. THIS IS WHAT INTERESTS MOST HUMANS

We human beings have a lot in common. We all share the same hopes, fears, needs, and desires. Stories that demonstrate those shared interests will be interesting to most of us. Fortunately, there are millions of such stories all around us all the time. They are all potential feature stories.

How to Write Profiles

1. A PROFILE IS A FEATURE STORY THAT ENTERTAINS AND INFORMS READERS BY TELLING THEM ENOUGH ABOUT A PERSON SO THAT THEY FEEL THEY KNOW THE SUBJECT

Profiles are among the most commonly attempted feature stories. Whatever new media may emerge, it is likely they will include profiles. When a writer succeeds in writing a true personality profile, the readers feel that they know the subject well. To accomplish this, the writer has to interview not only the subject but also several people who know the subject well. The profile should include the subject's strengths and weaknesses, quirks and habits, and motivation. The profile should include information that makes the reader say, "Oh, so that's why he did that!" or "Now I understand why she is like that."

2. A PROFILE INCLUDES ALL THE SIGNIFICANT VITAL STATISTICS ABOUT THE SUBJECT, SUCH AS AGE, HEIGHT, WEIGHT, GENDER, RACE, RELIGION, OCCUPATION, AND APPEARANCE

There are many differences between profiles and hard news stories. When a person is mentioned in a typical news story, there is usually no reason to include information about the person's appearance or family situation. For example, a responsible reporter would never write that "the suspect was arrested by Officer Janice Smith, a petite blonde who was divorced recently."

However, if the reporter were writing a personality profile of Officer Janice Smith, then her size, hair color, and marital status all would be important details to include. Perhaps the fact that her appearance is different from that of a typical police officer on the force will help readers to better understand her personality. Police work puts a strain on many marriages. Was her divorce related to her job? Readers can read the whole profile and decide for themselves.

News coverage should be fair, unbiased, and free from prejudice, but that does not mean that journalists always must omit telling details. Prejudice involves making judgments before collecting all the relevant information, and that makes for bad journalism. Writing profiles involves collecting as much of the relevant information as possible, and that makes for good information.

The information in a profile should be specific—the more specific, the better. Instead of saying that the person is tall, tell us how tall. Instead of saying that the person is thin, include the height and weight. Instead of calling the person "jovial," include an anecdote in which the person tells a joke.

3. A PROFILE INCLUDES ENOUGH COMMENTS ABOUT THE SUBJECT FROM OTHER PEOPLE SO THAT THE READERS FEEL THEY KNOW THE SUBJECT WELL

If you ask a person to "tell me about yourself," you will get a very limited view. Most people will paint a picture of themselves as being rather ordinary. They probably will not describe themselves in highly complimentary or highly critical ways.

However, if you ask people's friends, colleagues, and relatives to describe them, you will get a goldmine of quotable comments.

4. A PROFILE INCLUDES ENOUGH DIRECT QUOTATIONS FROM THE SUBJECT SO THAT THE READERS GET A FEEL FOR THE SUBJECT'S SPEECH PATTERNS AND PERSONALITY

Although quotations about the subject of a profile should come from others, it is also important to include direct quotations from the subject. Nice, long quotes that capture the rhythm of the person's speech pattern are wonderful components of a profile. There is no need to use direct quotations for simple statements of fact, such as, "I was born in Arkansas."

However, if the subject tosses out a colloquial expression, go for it: "When I was a young'n, I was hell-bent on being a fiddle player in a bluegrass band, but you cain't hardly put bacon on the table that-a-way."

5. A REPORTER WRITING A PROFILE SHOULD TALK TO FRIENDS AND ACQUAINTANCES BOTH BEFORE AND AFTER INTERVIEWING THE SUBJECT OF THE PROFILE

It helps to talk to the subject's friends before interviewing the subject so that you have some background for the interview. It always helps to say, "Your friend Larry told me you went to Woodstock. What was that like?"

Then, after the interview, you probably will have more questions for the person's friends.

6. A PROFILE SHOULD SHOW THE SUBJECT IN ACTION

A good profile will describe the person doing something. For example, a profile of Jesse Jackson, Jr., by Jennifer Loven of the Associated Press describes the congressman standing on the shore of Lake Michigan:

> Brandishing a piece of driftwood, he bellows at the prosperous Loop's distant skyline: "Let the South Side of Chicago go!"

Even small touches such as "Leaning back in his desk chair with his hands behind his head . . ." or "Drumming on the dashboard to the beat of a song on her car radio . . ." can give the reader a glimpse of the person's personality.

7. A PROFILE MUST HAVE A FOCUS. A PROFILE SHOULD HAVE ONE MAIN POINT, AND IT SHOULD BE STATED CLEARLY IN A "NUT GRAF"

People's personalities are complex and multifaceted. In order to make a profile readable, the writer must choose one aspect of the person's personality and make it the dominant theme of the article. This doesn't mean that the profile can say only one thing but that it should be organized around one unifying theme.

It is important to make that one theme abundantly clear in the first few paragraphs. Otherwise, the readers may begin to wonder why they are bothering to read the article.

8. NO PROFILE SHOULD BE ENTIRELY POSITIVE OR ENTIRELY NEGATIVE BECAUSE PEOPLE ARE MORE COMPLEX THAN THAT

Profiles should have one main theme, but they should not be one-dimensional. If everything you have learned is complimentary, or if everything you learned is critical, then you need to keep interviewing. Somewhere out there is a person who will provide an opposing point of view. The readers will find the profile more credible if there is a mixture of positive and negative comments about the person.

My friend Susan Goldstein told me this story from the days when she worked at the *Montachusett Review* in Fitchburg, Mass., between 1977 and 1982:

I was working for a tiny weekly newspaper that had no budget and hardly any staff (so it was a great training ground). The famous journalist George Plimpton was coming to our local ice arena to play with the Bruin's hockey team; somehow, our little paper got an exclusive interview. The editor sent two green reporters, myself and another one, over to the arena where we nervously interviewed who we considered the absolute "King of Journalism" (trying hard to act like we knew what we were doing) and snapping photographs with a Polaroid camera (that's the only kind of camera the newspaper could afford). Here's the sad part: After going through an elaborate production to set up the shot, we actually had no film in the camera. Of course with a Polaroid, you know right away. We snapped a photo of Plimpton skating on the ice in his hockey uniform and no film ejected. We had also neglected to carry any extra packets with us. We told Plimpton to wait and we rushed back to the newsroom, picked up another roll of film, loaded the camera, rushed back and asked him to skate again while we snapped his photo, but again, nothing happened. For some reason, the film itself was a bust. Do you think we thought to bring an extra pack with us? No, of course not. We asked Plimpton to wait yet again while we rushed back to the newsroom and picked up a second package of film. Unbelievably, he was still skating around the ice, patiently waiting for us when we returned. We did finally get his photograph and he smiled, never once complaining about our "green" reporting skills. We learned a good lesson that day: carry extras of any piece of equipment that's critical, from pencils to film (or batteries for today's photographers).

How to Market Feature Stories

1. WRITE EVERY DAY. TO BE A WRITER, YOU MUST WRITE. TO BE A SUCCESSFUL FREELANCE WRITER, YOU MUST SEND QUERIES AND ARTICLES OUT AGAIN AND AGAIN

Although most news stories are written by staff reporters, many feature stories are written by freelance writers. In the Middle Ages, knights who were not steadily employed by a lord were free to rent themselves out to the highest bidder. They would use their lance to fight for their latest employer and then, perhaps, move on to another lord for the next battle. Such is the life of a freelance writer, a writer who attempts to sell articles—usually feature stories—to various publications.

To be a successful freelance writer, you must go into battle every day. There are far more writers than opportunities for publication, so you must be persistent in your pursuit of publication. Even excellent stories by excellent writers get rejected because the articles do not happen to meet the needs of the publication to which they were submitted.

It is very difficult to make a living as a freelance writer. Many freelance writers have other jobs that give them time for writing, such as teaching, or have spouses who provide the dependable income and benefits.

2. SEND EITHER A QUERY LETTER DESCRIBING YOUR PROPOSED ARTICLE OR A COVER LETTER ATTACHED TO YOUR ARTICLE. YOUR QUERY OR COVER LETTER SHOULD BE PERFECT, AND SHORTER THAN ONE PAGE

The conventional wisdom of freelancing dictates that you must send a query letter to an editor first. This letter sells your proposed article by briefly describing the story and your qualifications for writing it. This query letter must be short and to the point. If it contains any errors or poor writing, those eliminate your chance of selling the story. Because it would be a waste of time to write the whole article without knowing that an editor is interested, most freelancers prefer this method.

Some magazines specify in their writers' guidelines that they prefer to receive queries rather than finished manuscripts. Newspapers are more likely than magazines to be amenable to receiving finished stories.

In this situation, the editor is likely to glance at the letter and then read the first two or three sentences of the story. If those first few words do not catch the editor's attention, the whole package gets tossed in the trash.

3. WHEN YOU SEND AN ARTICLE, IT SHOULD BE DOUBLE-SPACED AND IN 10- OR 12-POINT TYPE. PUT YOUR NAME ON EVERY PAGE

Although you may end up sending your article in digital form, the editor may want to see a printed copy first. That printed copy should be designed for easy reading. Most editors prefer 12-point type. Double-space the lines, leave 1-inch margins all around, and use a standard typeface such as Times New Roman.

It also helps to leave a lot of space at the top of the first page. Starting the text halfway down the first page leaves room for the editor to make a notation in pencil and pass it along to another editor for consideration. If the editor wants to make a note such as, "Look at this wonderful feature story," you will want to be sure that he or she has plenty of room to write that.

4. QUERY LETTERS MUST BE BRIEF AND INTERESTING. INCLUDE WHO YOU ARE, WHAT YOUR EXPERTISE IS, WHAT YOUR IDEA IS, WHY YOUR STORY IS UNIQUE, AND WHO THE SOURCES ARE. INCLUDE YOUR PHONE NUMBER

If you have an idea for an article and find a publication that you think might be interested, send a letter or e-mail to the appropriate editor, often the managing editor or assistant managing editor. The top editors listed in the publication's masthead probably are too busy to read your letter, so send it to one of their assistants. The goal of the query letter is to get the editor to say, "Yes, I am interested in your article." The query must be catchy and interesting. If editors detect any weakness in your writing, they will not respond positively. A mistake in spelling, punctuation, or grammar is the kiss of death.

The query letter should describe the subject of the article and tell why it is right for that particular publication. Explain why you are the right person to write it. If you have any expertise in the subject or any unique contacts, be sure to mention them. This is no time to be modest.

You should make it as easy as possible for the editor to contact you. One way is to include a stamped, self-addressed envelope. In this way, an interested editor simply can scribble, "Yes, I am interested in your article," on the bottom of your query and mail it back to you. Also include your telephone number and e-mail address so that the editor can contact you that way.

It helps to mention that you would be happy to send the story by e-mail or on disk and ask what format the editor prefers. Be careful about e-mail correspondence. Most people tend to write in a much more casual style when sending e-mail. If you do send an e-mail note to an editor, make sure that you plan, write, edit, and proofread it as carefully as you would a traditional letter. E-mail correspondence is much faster than old-fashioned "snail mail," and a poorly written e-mail can destroy a writer's reputation with amazing speed.

5. IT IS IMPORTANT TO INCLUDE CLIPS OF YOUR PUBLISHED STORIES. THIS LETS THE EDITOR SEE YOUR WORK AND LETS THE EDITOR KNOW THAT OTHER EDITORS HAVE USED YOUR WORK. DO NOT EXPECT TO GET THESE CLIPS BACK

Clips are photocopies of published articles clipped out of publications. Whenever you publish an article in a newspaper or magazine, be sure to cut it out, indicate the date and name of publication, and make several photocopies of it, preferably fitting it onto standard 8½-by-11-inch paper. The original clippings are likely to fade and yellow, particularly if they are printed on newsprint. The photocopies will last longer, especially if they are kept in a closed file cabinet. A good set of clips is a writer's best asset.

When applying for a job or sending a query letter, be sure to include about three of these clips. Editors who see that you have had work published before will be more likely to take a chance on you because they can see that you have had the experience of working with another editor.

6. KNOW THE PUBLICATION. YOU NEED TO READ THE PUBLICATION FOR WHICH YOU WANT TO WRITE. NOTE THE LENGTHS, SUBJECTS, TONE, AND VOICE OF THE ARTICLES THE EDITORS BUY. FIGURE OUT THE TARGET AUDIENCE, AND WRITE FOR THAT AUDIENCE

The most common reason an editor rejects an article is that it is not appropriate for the publication. Therefore, before trying to sell your story to a publication, study that publication. Make sure that you know the kinds of articles it prints. Make sure that your article is the same length, style, and general subject area of articles the publication already has published. Also make sure that your article does not duplicate something the publication already has published.

For example, *Yankee* magazine publishes articles about people, places, and events in the six New England states: Maine, New Hampshire, Vermont, Massachusetts, Connecticut, and Rhode Island. The greatest article in the world about skiing in the

Adirondacks will never make it in *Yankee* because the Adirondack Mountains of New York are not in New England.

7. LEARN TO THINK LIKE AN EDITOR. THE EDITOR HAS CERTAIN SLOTS TO FILL IN THE MAGAZINE'S FORMAT. STUDY THE FORMAT OF THE MAGAZINE. LOOK FOR REGULAR DEPARTMENTS AND STANDING FEATURES. COPY THE FORMAT OF THE MAGAZINE

Newspapers and magazines are supported by advertising. So the size of the publication is determined by the amount of advertising sold. Once that basic decision is made, editors begin to fill in the space between the ads with a regular series of standard features. (In this case, the word *features* is used to mean any regularly appearing type of content.)

In a monthly magazine, for instance, there might always be letters to the editor, some regular personal columnists, an advice column, a pictorial, a first-person story, a personality profile, and a major investigative story.

The *Washington Monthly,* for example, covers politics, government, and the media. They publish, among other things, book reviews of recent political and cultural titles that are usually about 800 words. If you send them a 2,000-word book review, it won't fit into their format.

8. READ AND FOLLOW THE WRITERS' GUIDELINES OR CONTRIBUTORS' GUIDELINES FOR THE PUBLICATION YOU ARE TARGETING

Most magazines and some newspapers publish formal guidelines for freelance writers. These are available on request and usually are also published on the magazine's Web site. They usually spell out exactly the kind of articles the publication seeks and how to submit them.

9. USE WRITER'S MARKET TO RESEARCH THE MARKET FOR FREELANCE ARTICLES

Writer's Market is an annual book published by *Writer's Digest* magazine. It lists thousands of publications that buy articles from freelance writers. It is also available in an online version for a fee. The printed book is available at most public libraries. The entries include basic guidelines for the publications and indicate to whom you should address your queries. It also includes information about payment and rights. It is organized and indexed so that you can look at similar publications and decide which are most appropriate for the subject you have in mind.

10. ONE OF THE BIGGEST MARKETS TODAY IS IN SERVICE ARTICLES, SUCH AS WHERE TO GO, WHAT TO DO, HOW TO SAVE MONEY, OR WHERE TO FIND NEEDED INFORMATION. HOT TOPICS ARE HEALTH CARE, HOUSE AND GARDEN, AND PERSONAL FINANCE. SEE WHAT SUBJECTS THE EDITORS FAVOR

There are trends in popular articles, but at the beginning of the twenty-first century, most newspapers and magazines seemed to like service articles. These are articles that provide useful information to consumers. A catchy way to write one of these service articles is to make it into a numbered list. You are likely to see articles entitled, "Ten Ways to Save Money on Your Next Vacation," "Five Easy Ways to Improve Your Diet," or "Fifteen Ways to Improve Your Sex Life."

11. THINK AHEAD. LOOK 6 TO 12 MONTHS AHEAD FOR PUBLISHING IN MAGAZINES. SEND CHRISTMAS STORIES IN JUNE. SEND VACATION STORIES IN DECEMBER

Editors buy freelance stories well in advance. Newspapers may plan special feature sections a few months in advance and news stories a few weeks in advance. Magazines work even further in advance, often 6 to 12 months ahead. The writers' guidelines often mention these timetables.

12. PAY FOR MAGAZINE ARTICLES VARIES WIDELY

Beginning writers often accept whatever pay they can get because getting a published clip helps their career. After you have gained some experience, you will want to negotiate your rate of pay. Large national magazines pay more than small regional magazines, and newspapers pay even less.

Recent estimates range from 10 cents per word to $2 per word. Most magazine articles are 500 to 2,000 words. Newspapers typically pay about $50 to $200 per article; magazines typically pay about $100 to $1,000 per article. Well-known writers can command even higher prices from the best magazines.

13. FIND OUT WHAT "RIGHTS" THEY WANT TO BUY. YOU HAVE A RIGHT TO NEGOTIATE

Usually, you sell *first-time rights* to a publication, and you retain the right to republish your article elsewhere. Get advice from National Writers Union or *Writer's Digest* magazine and its annual edition called *Writer's Market*. The field of electronic rights or Web rights is evolving quickly, and you should decide whether you want to grant someone the right to publish your article on the Internet.

In some situations the publisher can copyright material published on the Internet, and in other circumstances the writer can hold the copyright, but as a practical matter, writers should be aware that, once written material appears on the Internet, many people feel free to copy it and redistribute it in an infinite variety of ways. Even though redistribution of copyrighted material is a violation of federal law, it is commonplace.

14. IT HELPS TO DEVELOP A PERSONAL RELATIONSHIP WITH AN EDITOR

Most successful freelance writers have personal relationships with a few editors who publish their work regularly. An editor is likely to purchase an article from someone he or she knows and trusts rather than from a stranger. So it helps tremendously to cultivate that kind of friendship.

15. FIND OUT WHAT FORM, FORMAT, AND DELIVERY METHOD IS PREFERRED BY THE EDITOR WITH WHOM YOU ARE DEALING

Some editors prefer to receive feature stories on paper, some by e-mail, either as plain text or in an attachment. Some may want a CD or other memory medium containing your story. Some may want to have you paste your story onto a Web-based form. These preferences are changing with increasing speed in the twenty-first century, so it is worth checking with the editor by phone or e-mail.

16. EXPLORE THE EMERGING WORLD OF NEW MEDIA FOR FREELANCE OPPORTUNITIES

New media are emerging rapidly, particularly in the years since the new millennium. These new means of mass communication, including Web sites, blogs, e-zines, and podcasts, need content. Traditional media, such as newspapers, magazines, and radio and television stations also seek additional content for their Web sites and other new projects. Pay varies widely for work in these media, but it is worth exploring. New technology has also expanded possibilities for telecommuting or working at home for a medium in a distant location and sending work in electronically. Many magazines now employ copy editors who work far from the magazine's headquarters.

How Newspapers Are Organized

Despite the recent dramatic changes in the news media, most news writing is done for newspapers. In order to understand how news stories are handled, it helps to understand the organization for which you are writing. The distinct separation between news and advertising, for example, is a function of both the editorial policy and the organizational structure of most good newspapers. The organizational structure of other news media is usually based on the newspaper model.

1. AS A BUSINESS, A NEWSPAPER IS TYPICALLY ORGANIZED INTO ABOUT NINE OR TEN DEPARTMENTS

- The administrative, executive, or general management department is headed by the publisher. If the publication is owned by a group or chain, the real power may reside in the corporate headquarters, and the on-site manager is an employee of the overall company. In other situations, the local publisher is the true chief executive officer.
- The news (or editorial) department is headed by the editor. Sometimes this person is given the title *editor-in-chief* to distinguish him or her from other editors. Occasionally, the publisher will take on the title *editor and publisher* to indicate a greater involvement in the editorial department. In that case, the *managing editor* is usually in charge of the editorial department.
- The retail or display advertising department is headed by the *retail advertising manager.* Graphic designers who produce the advertising may fall under one of the advertising departments or under the production department.
- The classified advertising department is headed by the *classified advertising manager.* This department includes the people who accept, design, and place classified advertising. Classified advertising in newspapers has declined precipitously in the early twenty-first century.
- The circulation or customer service department is headed by the *circulation manager.* This department takes care of distribution to subscribers through a network of carriers, who are likely to be independent contractors. The department also handles distribution of papers to retail outlets.

- The production department is headed by the *production manager.* This department usually includes a variety of workers who actually produce the newspapers.
- The business or accounting department is headed by the *business manager* or *comptroller.* This department typically handles payroll for employees, billing for subscribers and advertisers, payment of the newspaper's bills, and other business functions.
- The building and maintenance department is headed by the *building super-intendent.* This may be called the *facilities department* or *physical plant department,* and it usually handles maintenance and security of the buildings, equipment, and vehicles.
- The personnel or human resources department is headed by the *human resources manager.* This department takes care of maintaining personnel records and complying with state and federal regulations concerning employment, compensation, benefits, retirement, and taxes.
- New technology, new ventures, and online operations may be handled by an entirely separate department or may be handled by existing departments.

2. WITHIN THE NEWS OR EDITORIAL DEPARTMENT, ONE OR TWO MANAGING EDITORS AND A NUMBER OF OTHER EDITORS USUALLY ASSIST THE EDITOR

News writers are concerned primarily with the news department, housed in a room or group of offices informally called the *newsroom.* The head honcho here is called the *editor-in-chief,* the *editor,* the *executive editor,* or the *managing editor.* Often the editor has one, two, or more managing editors to divide up the supervisory duties.

Working under them are a variety of editors, which may include:

- City editor
- Metro editor
- State editor
- News editor
- Business editor
- Sports editor
- Graphics editor
- Photo editor
- Features editor
- Sunday editor
- Entertainment editor
- Special sections editor
- Copy desk chief
- Design desk chief
- Online or Web editor

These hands-on editors assign stories, edit copy, lay out pages, and make decisions about what the newspaper should cover and how it should be covered. They usually meet in news meetings or budget meetings once or twice a day to discuss plans for the next edition.

These editors may have a variety of assistant editors, including a staff of copy editors and page designers. Some of the editors, typically the city editor or the metro editor, supervise a staff of reporters and, in some cases, bureau chiefs in other locations. The graphics or photo editor supervises a staff of photographers and graphic artists.

3. THE INFORMATION PUBLISHED IN THE NEWSPAPER IS DIVIDED INTO SEVERAL CATEGORIES

Another way of looking at the newspaper's organization is to look at the content rather than the personnel who work there. Often the organizational structure is parallel, but there are some differences.

- *News.* This includes hard news or breaking news, as well as investigative reporting, analysis, and news features, such as profiles and human interest stories.
- *Features.* This includes feature stories, such as entertainment stories; reviews; trend stories; fashion, food, and how-to stories; and amusements, such as comics, advice columns, puzzles, games, and television and movie schedules.
- *Opinion.* This includes editorials (which are the official position of the newspaper's editorial board), opinion columns, political columns, personal columns, humor columns, letters to the editor, and political cartoons.
- *Advertising.* This includes blocks of the newspaper pages sold to advertisers to display in words and graphics their products or services.

4. THE DIVISION BETWEEN NEWS AND FEATURES IS VAGUE, AND BOTH COME FROM THE EDITORIAL DEPARTMENT

Reporters and editors in the newsroom work on both news stories and feature stories, sometimes mixing the two. Sometimes a reporter will describe a potential story to a hard news editor, such as a city editor, and the city editor will say, "You better go pitch that to Features." In such a case, the reporter is free to talk to the features editor, who may suggest it to the lifestyle, entertainment, or arts editor.

If a reporter were covering a play to write a review for the features department and was at the theater when it caught fire, the features editor probably would advise the reporter to pitch the fire story to the news department.

5. IN GOOD NEWSPAPERS, OPINION IS CLEARLY LABELED AND SEPARATED FROM NEWS, ALTHOUGH IT ALSO COMES FROM THE EDITORIAL DEPARTMENT

The separation between news and opinion is—or should be—much more distinct. In good newspapers, opinions should appear only on the opinion pages, and they should be clearly identified as such. News stories do not belong on those pages, and opinion pieces do not belong on news pages. Most newspapers also forbid reporters covering a news story from writing opinion columns about the same subject. Readers might doubt the reporter's objectivity if the reporter expressed an opinion on one page and attempted to present an objective news story on another page.

Yet both the news pages and the opinion pages are under the jurisdiction of the paper's editor, who makes sure that the writing on both is clear, accurate, fair, and balanced. The opinions on the editorial pages are supposed to be informed opinions based on information provided on the news pages.

Before the 1960s, most newspapers had only one opinion page, typically called the *editorial page* because it included the editorials, which are unsigned expressions of the paper's editorial opinion. Then some newspapers, most notably *The New York Times,* decided to use the next page to present more opinions, including some that were directly opposed to the opinions expressed in the editorials. Since this page was both physically and philosophically opposite the editorial page, it became known as the *op/ed page.*

6. IN GOOD NEWSPAPERS, THE DIVISION BETWEEN THE PRODUCTS OF THE EDITORIAL DEPARTMENT AND THE PRODUCTS OF THE ADVERTISING DEPARTMENT IS SHARP AND DISTINCT

It is customary to say there is a "brick wall" between news and advertising. Advertising should be completely and clearly separated from all editorial content because the content of advertising is controlled by the advertiser rather than by the newspaper's editor.

Cynics point out accurately that more than 90 percent of the revenue of a typical newspaper comes from advertising, so it is logical to assume that editors would never permit anything to appear in the news pages that would offend an advertiser. The same cynics also point out that publishing is itself a big business, so it is logical to assume that editors would never print anything that would offend big business in general.

The truth is not this simple. Although the pressure of advertising and big business may have some influence on the decisions made by reporters and editors, any overt influence of that sort is considered unethical and is discouraged at most newspapers in North America. Reporters and editors are taught in journalism classes to resist any influence by advertisers. Newspapers stake their reputation on presenting objective, unbiased information. This is why readers buy the newspapers. If people stopped believing the objectivity of the news stories, they would stop buying the paper, and that, in turn, would hurt the advertisers.

> When I was Sunday editor of the Cape Cod Times, I assigned a reporter to write a story about a helpful new agency called the Consumer Assistance Council. The story began with an anecdote about a consumer who had a dispute with a car dealer.
>
> On Monday morning I got a call from the car dealer. He said it made him look bad. He wanted me to run a feature the following Sunday that made him look good.
>
> I asked if there was anything incorrect in the story that ran.
>
> No, he said, the facts were all correct, but it made him look unreasonable and he didn't like it, and he demanded a flattering article the next Sunday.
>
> "If there were any errors of fact, we will run a correction, but otherwise there is nothing we can do for you," I told him.
>
> He then asked me to look at the back of the last section of the Sunday newspaper, where there was a full-page ad for his dealership. He asked if I knew he was one of the

newspaper's largest advertisers. I did. He asked if I knew how much money he paid for his ads. I did not.

"That's a completely separate department, sir," I said.

At that point he demanded to speak to the publisher.

So I transferred him to Scott Himstead, the publisher of the *Cape Cod Times*.

The next day I saw the publisher in the hallway and nervously inquired about the call.

"Yeah, he told me you said, 'If there were any errors of fact, we will run a correction, but otherwise there is nothing we can do for you,'" the publisher related to me.

"And what did you say?"

"I said, 'As our Sunday editor told you, if there were any errors of fact, we will run a correction, but otherwise there is nothing we can do for you.'"

The car dealer pulled all his advertising for a few weeks, but then he came back and ran even more ads.

Scott Himstead later told me that he was glad I acted independently with the best interest of the readers in mind. "That's what I hire editors for," he said.

7. TRADITIONAL MEDIA ARE REORGANIZING THEMSELVES TO REFLECT EMERGING NEW MEDIA

Traditional news media—especially newspapers and magazines—are embracing new technology by transforming themselves into information suppliers on various platforms. Different models are being tried to accommodate these new roles. Most continue to use the same basic organizational structure with the addition of a new department to oversee new media.

At almost every newspaper in America, reporters and editors who once concerned themselves solely with getting stories in print in the next day's edition now submit stories to their newspaper's online edition. Often this is done under the direction of an online editor who reports to the editor-in-chief. Many reporters publish blogs, and in 2010 many newspapers began participating in social networking sites, such as Twitter and Facebook.

How to Plan a Newspaper

A good news writer should understand the editorial process in whatever medium is being used. For example, editors may need your story long before the paper is printed. If you are not aware of all the steps involved in putting out a newspaper, radio broadcast, television broadcast, Web site, blog, podcast, or other news medium, you might not understand why this is necessary.

This chapter is based on the assumption that you are the hands-on editor of a small newspaper and that you have a role in every step of the process. At most newspapers, of course, different people or different departments handle various steps of this process. The same general process takes place at every newspaper, whether it is the *Wall Street Journal* or a community college student weekly. A similar process is used in any news medium.

1. FIRST, THINK ABOUT GOALS, OBJECTIVES, AND PURPOSES. WHAT ARE WE TRYING TO ACHIEVE?

Before touching a computer, telephone, or notebook, a good editor (or news director at a broadcast outlet) will stop and think. If you don't have a clear idea of where you want to go, you will never get there. At a daily newspaper, your goal may be almost exactly the same every day, in which case you need only remind yourself of that goal.

Each day brings new objectives, however. After a major news event, an editor may decide to give readers all the information the reporters can find about the causes of the event or the results of the event or both. Another editor may decide to get ahead of the story by asking what will happen next.

2. MAKE UP A STORY LIST. WHAT ARTICLES DO WE WANT, AND WHICH OF THEM CAN WE GET?

At most news media, the list of stories is called a *news budget*. Some stories on the list may be stories that are already written and waiting to be printed. Others may be assigned stories that are still being prepared. Still others may be stories the editors want but have not yet assigned. Information about the status of each story should be included on the list. At some papers, story lists are just scribbled on paper; at others, they are computer files. At very small operations, one editor keeps the budget for the entire paper, but at most papers the task is divided up by department.

Once or twice a day at dailies, editors gather for a meeting to plan the next edition. These meetings are often called *budget meetings, news meetings,* or *planning meetings.* Everyone with a news budget brings it to these meetings so that everyone can discuss what stories are available.

3. MAKE UP A PHOTO LIST. WHAT PHOTOGRAPHS WILL ILLUSTRATE THE STORIES? WHAT PHOTOGRAPHS WILL TELL STORIES THEMSELVES?

Whenever a story is assigned, someone should consider whether an accompanying photograph also should be assigned. Other photographs are assigned or simply taken by photographers who see a good shot. All these are collected in a *photo budget.* Usually a photo or graphics editor brings this list to the planning meetings.

4. PLAN ANY ONLINE OR MULTIMEDIA COMPONENTS FOR THE STORY

Depending on the degree to which the newspaper has an online component, this could be as simple as planning to post the print story on the Web site or as complicated as assigning video, audio, or interactive content. In some cases, editors may want to use the Web site to promote future content, either on the Web site or in the print edition. In some cases, editors may want to assign someone to compile a list of Web-based resources to complement the story in print.

5. DELEGATE RESPONSIBILITIES. CHOOSE EDITORS TO TAKE RESPONSIBILITY FOR VARIOUS AREAS

No one editor can put out an entire newspaper alone. A good leader will delegate responsibility to other people. If a big story is breaking, a good lead editor will put someone in charge of making sure that that story is covered properly. Most news editors, for example, will delegate all sports stories to the purview of the sports editor.

6. MAKE SPECIFIC ASSIGNMENTS. ASSIGN STORIES, PHOTOS, AND OTHER TASKS

Once it is decided that a particular story is needed, an assigning editor must assign it to a reporter and, if applicable, a photographer. In some cases, a graphic artist may be assigned to make a map, chart, or graphic of some sort. The assigning editor has to make sure that these people follow through and finish their tasks before deadline.

Editing, layout, design, and production tasks also have to be given to specific people with specific deadlines. The whole paper cannot be done at once, so some sections may have to be completed earlier than others. In a typical Sunday newspaper, for example, the feature sections, such as travel and entertainment, may be completed earlier in the week. The front page and the sports section front, covering the latest news, are usually completed at the last possible hour.

7. COORDINATE THE PARTS. MAKE SURE THAT THE REPORTERS, PHOTOGRAPHERS, AND EDITORS ARE WORKING TOGETHER

It is usually the job of a managing editor to make sure that everything comes together. Although journalists are in the communications business, there are frequent communications problems in a newsroom. A good coordinator needs to make sure that the proverbial right hand knows what the left hand is doing. For example, if a famous athlete is arrested, someone needs to make sure that the same story does not appear in both the news and sports pages. If a photographer is getting a shot of this athlete's arraignment, someone has to make sure that the editor laying out the page knows that the photograph is coming.

8. COLLECT YOUR MATERIAL. ENFORCE DEADLINES, AND DO WHAT IS NECESSARY TO GET THE STORIES, GRAPHICS, AND PHOTOS YOU NEED

Deadlines are extremely important in journalism. News must be timely, so things may be done at the last minute, but the definition of just when that last minute is must be clear to everyone working on the story. An assignment editor must be firm in telling the reporter and photographer, "You must get that to us by 9 P.M." or "If you don't have it to us by 9 P.M., it's not running." Sometimes the editor has to decide to run a story even if certain parts are missing. There is always a balancing act between speed and completeness.

9. CAREFULLY EDIT YOUR COPY AND ART. MAKE SURE THAT IT IS AS GOOD AS POSSIBLE. IF IT IS NOT ACCEPTABLE, DO NOT USE IT

Once the story and art (which is newsroom jargon for photographs and illustrations) are handed in, they must be edited. Everything must be checked for accuracy, completeness, and proper style. There are times when an editor may look over a story and decide that it is better than expected and should be considered for "better play," such as running on page one. There are other times when the story may be worse than expected and should not be printed at all.

10. WHEN IT'S DEADLINE TIME, GO WITH WHAT YOU HAVE. DO NOT LEAVE BLANKS, HOPING THAT SOMETHING BETTER WILL COME IN LATE. USE THE CREAM OF THE CROP

Just as reporters have to stop collecting information and write when the deadline approaches, editors have to stop collecting stories and lay out the newspaper when the deadline approaches. Leaving a space for a late-breaking story is a dangerous practice because that late story may not materialize. It is a much safer option to fill the space with a story that can be deleted if the better one does come along before it is too late.

11. WRITE LIVELY, INTERESTING HEADLINES AND CUTLINES THAT TELL THE STORY QUICKLY AND ACCURATELY

At most publications, headlines are written by copy editors or page designers, not reporters. A good headline will summarize the whole story in four to eight words. It also will let the readers know whether they want to read more of the story (see Chapter 29).

Cutlines in a newspaper appear next to a photograph to explain its newsworthiness. They are usually written by the photographer and then passed along to a copy editor, who will improve the cutline after editing any related stories and seeing how the photograph is displayed on the page (see Chapter 30).

12. LOOK FOR LEAD STORY AND LEAD ART. IF THEY ARE ON THE SAME SUBJECT, THAT'S EVEN BETTER

Every edition of every publication should have one article that is its best offering. That article is called the *lead story*. There also should be one photograph or other illustration that is the best of the edition. This is the *lead art*. In the best of all possible worlds, the two are on the same subject, and then you have a package of a great story with an accompanying great illustration. If they do not go together, it is usually possible to lay out the front page in such a way that the lead story and lead art are both visible at the top of page one.

13. SORT THE STORIES ACCORDING TO PAGE—"A PLACE FOR EVERYTHING AND EVERYTHING IN ITS PLACE"

At some point early in the planning process, an editor must go through the story list and photo list and assign each to a page. The best, of course, will go on page one. Related stories should be placed together. The whole pattern should make it easy for readers to find what they want. This organizational effort should begin long before stories are actually placed on pages.

By the way, if related stories cannot be adjacent, they can be tied together by a note referring to the related story elsewhere in the paper. This note is called a *refer*, and it is sometimes spelled "reefer" because that is how it is pronounced in newsrooms. (So, naturally, a reference to a related story about people arrested with marijuana cigarettes would be called a "reefer reefer.")

14. SKETCH ROUGH LAYOUTS OF EACH PAGE. MAKE SURE THAT YOU HAVE ALL THE COPY AND ART YOU NEED

Once an editor has decided what is going on each page, someone—usually a copy editor or page designer—should draw a rough sketch of each page to plan a good presentation. Some computer programs allow you to do this on a computer. This sketch is called a *dummy*.

15. FINALLY, LAY OUT THE PAGES ON THE COMPUTER, REMEMBERING THAT THE COMPUTER IS YOUR TOOL, NOT YOUR MASTER

Journalism ain't computers, and computers ain't journalism. Benjamin Franklin is probably America's greatest journalist, and he never used a computer. Joseph Pulitzer and

William Randolph Hearst ran their competing newspaper empires without the benefit of computers. In fact, all journalists who put out newspapers before the 1960s did so without computers.

Of course, computers have made difficult tasks easy and impossible tasks possible for journalists, but it would be a mistake to assume that the first step in putting out a newspaper is booting up a computer. The first step involves thinking and setting priorities, something the human mind is particularly suited to and something a computer is not suited to. After making the decisions on a human level, people can use computers to make their tasks easier. Nowhere is this more apparent than in the process of newspaper design. Using newspaper design software, such as QuarkXPress or InDesign, is much easier than the old methods of pasting up strips of paper or arranging lead type. Nevertheless, a good journalist should remember that the purpose of the computer is to serve humans.

16. THERE ARE MANY WAYS TO FILL THE "NEWS HOLE" OF A NEWSPAPER

Most newspapers are designed to get larger (in number of pages) as the amount of advertising increases. The space to be filled by the editorial department after the advertising is placed is known as the *news hole*. Ideally, the locally produced news and feature stories and photographs, combined with standing features and opinion pages, will exactly equal that space. But that rarely happens.

If you have too much copy for the news hole, select the most important and most timely material, and hold the rest. If you have too little copy to fill the news hole, there are several strategies to solve that problem. Increasing the size of photographs (within reason) often takes care of the problem. If your newspaper subscribes to a wire service, such as the Associated Press, then there is a virtually unlimited amount of copy there. Another source of copy is press releases, although it is important to have a reporter create an objective news story based on the press release, rather than simply printing a press release as it appears.

17. DOUBLE-CHECK EVERYTHING FOR ACCURACY BEFORE "PUTTING THE PAPER TO BED"

The last, and most important, step in planning a newspaper edition is to check everything as carefully as possible. This usually involves checking pages on computer screens before they are sent to composing and then checking printed copies (or *proofs*) of the pages after that. A good editor also will look at one of the first copies off the press and check every page carefully. One of the problems with computer technology is that things tend to look good on a computer screen; it is easy to overlook mistakes. Once it is printed on paper, some of those same mistakes are more obvious.

The old phrase "putting the paper to bed" comes from the days of a flat-bed press, when each page of a newspaper was placed on the bed of a printing press, and sheets of paper were pressed onto it. Today, the final steps in putting out a newspaper are still known as "putting it to bed," although it may involve nothing more than a simple click of a computer mouse.

How to Lay Out A Page

The average reader probably gives little or no thought to the subject of page design. This is a good thing. A well-designed page in a newspaper or magazine or on the Internet should draw attention to the content of the publication, not to the design itself. But a good journalist should have at least a basic understanding of page design in order to know how the process works.

For a more comprehensive discussion of newspaper page design, consult a good book on the subject. One of the best is *The Newspaper Designer's Handbook,* by Tim Harrower, published by McGraw-Hill.

1. THINK ABOUT GOALS, OBJECTIVES, AND PURPOSES. WHAT ARE YOU TRYING TO ACHIEVE?

This, of course, is the same as the first step in planning a newspaper (see Chapter 27) or almost any other enterprise. In laying out a page, it is important to pause first to see if there is any unifying theme to the page and keep that in mind when working on it.

2. MAKE UP A STORY LIST. WHAT ARTICLES DO YOU WANT, AND WHICH OF THEM CAN YOU GET?

Any page designer must have a complete list of stories and art for the page. It is a dangerous idea to leave a hole for a story that may or may not come in later. Work with what is in hand now. A quick sketch using rough estimates may help to determine whether you have too much stuff or not enough. Small adjustments can be made by enlarging a photograph or cutting a story. Larger problems have to be solved by adding or subtracting a story or photo.

3. MAKE UP A PHOTO LIST. WHAT PHOTOGRAPHS WILL ILLUSTRATE THE STORIES? WHAT PHOTOGRAPHS WILL TELL STORIES THEMSELVES?

Again, stick to what you have in hand now. Make a note of stories and photos that should be handled as a package. Photos that run without stories are called *free-standing art, stand-alones,* or *wild art.* They should be set off in a distinctive way, usually in a box.

4. CALCULATE THE APPROXIMATE LENGTH OF EACH STORY ON THE PAGE, AND WRITE IT DOWN

In some cases, the computer will tell you how long a story will be when placed on a page. In any case, you can make a rough estimate based on the number of words. Most newspaper columns are about 12 picas (2 inches) wide, and at that width, you get about 40 words per inch. So you can make a rough estimate that a 400-word article will be about 10 inches long. You need to be much more accurate later, but at first a rough estimate is good enough.

5. CROP THE GRAPHICS AND PHOTOS THAT YOU PLAN TO USE, AND NOTE THEIR SHAPE. WRITE DOWN THEIR PRESENT DIMENSIONS AS "ORIGINAL WIDTH AND DEPTH"

It helps to make printouts of any photographs you may use. It is often easier to look at photographs on paper than on a computer screen. Then you can put a ruler to each photo and note its width and depth. If you notice that there is a distracting area that clearly needs to be cropped out, note the width and depth of the remaining area. It is best to discuss any cropping of photos with the photographer or photo editor, when possible. You should not crop any photo if you have not read the story that goes with it.

6. COORDINATE THE PARTS. WHICH STORIES GO WITH WHICH PHOTOS? IS THERE SOMETHING IN THE SUBJECT THAT SUGGESTS A CERTAIN LAYOUT OR DESIGN?

Perhaps a story about a new flagpole can be in a tall, narrow package. A story about a stretch limousine might go in a horizontal package. Is there a photo that relates to two stories and could be placed between them? Bear in mind that people will look at photos and graphics first, then probably read the cutline of that photo, then the headline, and then the text of the story.

7. LOOK FOR THE LEAD STORY AND THE LEAD ART. IF THEY ARE ON THE SAME SUBJECT, THAT'S EVEN BETTER

Just as every publication has a lead photo and lead art (see Chapter 27), every page in the publication should have its own lead. If there is more than one photograph, the lead photo should be twice the size of the next largest photo. The lead story should be near the top of the page and should have the largest headline, inviting people to read it first.

8. DRAW A DUMMY WITH PENCIL AND PAPER; YOU MAY HAVE TO MAKE SEVERAL VERSIONS UNTIL YOU GET ONE THAT WORKS WELL

A page designer is both a journalist and an artist. First, make journalistic decisions about the relative importance of the stories and art on your page. Then make artistic decisions about the most attractive way to display them. This is best done by drawing a dummy with a pencil and paper. Yes, there are computer programs that will do this for you, but they tend to limit creativity, so they are best used on pages deep inside the newspaper.

9. START WITH YOUR LEAD STORY OR STORY-AND-ART PACKAGE, AND SKETCH A RECTANGULAR MODULE THAT WILL CONTAIN IT. THEN ADD OTHER RECTANGLES FOR EACH OTHER STORY OR STORY-AND-ART PACKAGE

Modular layout is the term used to describe a style of designing newspaper pages in which all the elements—such as headline, subhead, photo, story, quote, and graphic—are contained in a regular rectangle. Readers seem to like the orderly appearance created by neatly stacked rectangles. Modular layout came into fashion in the late 1960s, replacing layouts that were much more complicated and busy looking.

10. REMEMBER, YOU CAN MAKE A PHOTO LARGER OR SMALLER, BUT YOU CANNOT CHANGE ITS SHAPE

The general principal in sizing photographs is that the ratio of the width to the depth remains the same. Since you know the original width and depth, and you can choose how wide to make it (usually one, two, or three standard columns), you can determine the reproduction depth.

Of course, if you are using a modern newspaper design software package, the computer will do all this for you. Nevertheless, remembering the principles behind the system will make you a better designer. A tall, thin photo must remain a tall, thin photo regardless of its size (see Chapter 31).

11. REMEMBER TO LEAVE SPACE ABOVE EVERY STORY FOR A HEADLINE

A one-deck (one-line) 36-point headline takes up about half an inch. A two-deck 36-point headline takes up about 1 inch. Remember to leave space below every photograph for a cutline. Most cutlines take up about half an inch.

12. DO NOT PLACE TWO HEADLINES SIDE BY SIDE. THAT IS CALLED "KNOCKING HEADS"

One major principle of modular layout is that headlines should not be placed side by side. Usually it is possible to place a photograph next to a headline or use a different layout to avoid this problem. Other names for knocking heads include "butting heads" or "tombstoning." It should be avoided because the readers may get confused and read the two headlines together.

13. LAY OUT THE PAGES ON THE COMPUTER

Finally, after making a clear decision about how you want the page to look, it is time to use the computer program to do the final layout. Knowing in advance, for example, that you need to leave room for two photos at the bottom of the page will make it much easier to lay out the top half of the page. When all elements are in place, page designers adjust them to fit perfectly, making minor changes to the size and shape of the elements in a process popularly referred to in newsrooms as "tweaking" a page.

14. REMEMBER THAT THE COMPUTER IS YOUR TOOL, NOT YOUR MASTER

Computers can do many things for journalists, but a good editor will remember computers' limitations. If someone wants to know why you put a certain photo in a certain place, it should be for a human reason, not because a computer suggested it. A software program may suggest a simple, standard layout, but a human designer may want to break the rules and use a nonstandard layout for creative reasons. Design software may tell you that a story is too long, but a human designer will know whether it is a story that can be trimmed easily to fit. Spelling and grammar checking software may catch some mistakes, but such software is far from infallible. The computer will tell you if the headline fits and is spelled correctly, but it cannot tell you whether it captures the essence of the story.

How to Write Headlines

Reporters do not write the headlines for their own stories. Some newspapers encourage reporters to put "suggested heads" on top of their stories, but the real headline depends on the size and shape required by the layout of the page on which the story appears. A headline is as much a graphic device as it is content element. A good headline must fill the space allotted for it and look attractive on the page. After that, it must tell the essence of the story, attract attention to the story, and let the readers know whether they want to read the story. At most newspapers, headlines are written by copy editors who have edited the story and also know the layout of the page involved.

Headlines are not called "titles" because they serve a different purpose. Titles rarely tell the whole story; thus, "You can't judge a book by its cover." A good headline, in contrast, will tell the whole story. A reader should be able to judge a story by its headline.

1. SUMMARIZE THE STORY IN FOUR TO EIGHT WORDS. BE SURE THAT THE READER WILL KNOW WHAT THE STORY IS ABOUT BY READING THE HEADLINE

Headlines are written by copy editors or page designers at most publications. Standard headline sizes are selected so that the head can contain four to eight words. A headline of fewer than four words is usually too brief and requires more explanation. A headline of more than eight words is usually too wordy.

2. USE SUBJECT, VERB, AND OBJECT. USE THEM IN THAT ORDER (ACTIVE VOICE) WHENEVER POSSIBLE

Active voice is better than passive voice in almost all situations (see Chapter 11). This is especially true in headlines. Readers expect headlines to be succinct. Passive-voice constructions are particularly awkward in headlines. For example, "Judge shot by suspect" (passive) is not nearly as clear as "Suspect shoots judge" (active).

3. ALWAYS USE PRESENT TENSE

Although news stories frequently are written in the past tense, the headlines atop them should be in the present tense. This is just a convention adopted by newspapers. It may not be logical, but readers are used to it. No one would expect a headline to say, "Red Sox won World Series." Even though the game took place the previous night, the headline would be in present tense: "Red Sox win World Series." Thus, if the article says (in past tense), "Latvia invaded Lithuania yesterday," the headline would say (in present tense), "Latvia invades Lithuania."

4. OMIT ARTICLES (A, AN, AND THE) UNLESS THEY ARE ABSOLUTELY NECESSARY FOR UNDERSTANDING

Another convention of headline writing is to leave out certain words, primarily articles, such as *a*, *an*, and *the*. This is why you will never see a headline reading, "The Red Sox win the World Series" or "A suspect shoots a judge."

There is also a convention to omit the verb *to be* (including *is* and *are*) when it is possible to do so without ambiguity. For example, a headline could say "Jones elected chairman" instead of "Jones is elected chairman" or "Portland man missing" instead of "Portland man is missing." But a headline in the *Portland Oregonian* correctly read "Officer shot in Albuquerque is from Beaverton" because if the verb were omitted ("Officer shot in Albuquerque from Beaverton"), people might think that the bullet traveled from one city to the other.

5. USE COMMAS FOR AND. USE SEMICOLONS TO SEPARATE DIFFERENT THOUGHTS IN HEADLINES

Another headline convention is to use a comma instead of the word *and*. Thus a headline would read "Israelis, Palestinians agree to meet" rather than "Israelis and Palestinians agree to meet."

If a headline needs to convey two separate thoughts that ordinarily would be in separate sentences, a semicolon is used to separate them. An example would be "Reagan inaugurated; Iran frees hostages."

6. NEVER BREAK A WORD OVER TWO LINES; AVOID BREAKING A THOUGHT OVER TWO LINES

Words in headlines are never hyphenated to continue on a second line, as they might be in the text of a news story. Every word must be contained on one line. It is also a good idea to try to avoid breaking a thought over a line. This may be difficult with headlines over single-column stories, but it is a goal that makes reading easier. A thought or phrase that is divided awkwardly over two lines is called a *bad break*. An example of a bad break is something like

Terrorists blow
Up power plant

Readers tend to pause at the end of a line, so dividing the verbal phrase "blow up" on two lines makes it difficult to read. Since both lines of a two-deck headline should be about the same length, solving this problem is not easy. One solution might be

Terrorists destroy
Canal power plant

7. CAPITALIZE THE FIRST WORD AND PROPER NOUNS ONLY

Most newspapers use "down style" headlines, in which the only words of a headline that are capitalized are the first word and proper nouns. This matches the style of capitalization used in the text of the stories. A few newspapers—most notably *The New York Times*—still use "up style" headlines, in which all words, except articles, are capitalized.

8. MAKE THE HEADLINE APPROPRIATE TO THE TONE OF THE STORY

Because headlines should preview their stories, they should match the tone of the story. Use a humorous headline on humorous stories. Use serious headlines on serious stories. You can have fun with the head on a light feature, such as "Hula Hoops come around again" or "Oh have you seen the muffin man?" But a serious story always should be played straight.

9. USE STRONG VERBS. TRY FOR A VERB THAT INDICATES THE ACTION

Strong verbs are the backbone of all writing, including good headline writing. Unfortunately, the space limitations of headlines force copy editors into frequent use of particularly short words simply because they fit in the allotted space. Words such as *rip, mull, blast*, and *rift* are called "headlinese" because they are found much more often in headlines than in ordinary conversation. They should be avoided, if possible. Headlines with verbs that convey the meaning of the story are the best:

> Fire devastates Middletown family
> Restaurant dispute tears village apart
> Hailstorm pummels midstate area

10. HEADLINES ARE MEASURED IN POINTS

In the nineteenth century, when headlines were set with actual pieces of lead type, printers would buy fonts of type and keep them in large type drawers. They typically were available in standard sizes, measured in picas and points. There are 12 points in a pica and 6 picas in an inch. Headlines were usually 18, 24, 30, 36, 42, 48, or 60 points tall. Only in time of war or for a major breaking news story would a printer pull out the 72-point type, which has letters 1 inch tall.

The old measuring system of picas and points has survived into modern computer technology. The only difference is that you can now order up type of any size at all, including fractions of a point.

Most newspapers put larger headlines (60, 48, or 42 points) on lead stories. Medium-size heads (36, 30, or 24 points) typically go on small stories. Small heads (18, 14, or 12 points) typically go on briefs and sidebars. But every publication has its own headline style, which should be the guide for headline writers.

How to Write Cutlines

A *cutline* is a block of text describing a photograph. In journalism, cutlines are not called *captions*. A caption may identify the subject of a photograph, but a cutline also must make reference to the newsworthiness of the photo and completely identify everyone in it. Cutlines are usually written by the photographer and then passed along to a copy editor, who will improve the cutline after editing any related stories and seeing how the photograph is displayed on the page.

1. EVERY PHOTOGRAPH MUST HAVE A CUTLINE

Even if you think that the content of a photograph is obvious, some sort of cutline is required for every photograph. Do not assume that everyone knows your state's senior senator, for example. It is possible that a visitor from another country may be reading your newspaper and needs the identification. Those familiar with the person in the photograph will not object to seeing the person's name in the cutline.

2. NEVER ATTEMPT TO WRITE A CUTLINE WITHOUT LOOKING AT THE PHOTOGRAPH

This may sound obvious, but it happens all too frequently in newsrooms. Occasionally, page designers will attempt to plow ahead with a page while awaiting a photograph that isn't quite ready. So they try to write a cutline based on a rough description from a reporter or photographer. The next thing they know they have written a cutline that lists three names, but when the photograph appears, there are only two people in it.

The best way to write a cutline is to look carefully at the photograph and ask yourself what information the typical reader would want to know. If there is an object in the photograph that people might not recognize, explain what it is.

John and Mary Smith discuss the process of adoption during an interview in their Silver Spring home. The drawings in the background were drawn by Lisa, the 4-year-old girl they hope to adopt.

3. ALL PEOPLE IN PHOTOGRAPHS MUST BE IDENTIFIED WITH THEIR COMPLETE NAMES. IF THERE ARE SEVERAL PEOPLE, IDENTIFY THEM FROM LEFT TO RIGHT

In general, it is important to identify every person in a photograph. If you do not know the names of all the people, either find out or do not use the photograph. Newspapers are in the business of informing people, so they strive to identify everyone they picture.

There are a few exceptions to this rule. In group photographs, it is best to have no more than five people in the photograph and make sure that each face is at least the size of a dime when it is reproduced. Occasionally, it may be necessary to print a crowd shot, and in that case it is not necessary—or even possible—to identify each member. A cutline under a shot of the Mormon Tabernacle Choir performing or a shot of their audience does not need to include every name.

4. WRITE CUTLINES IN COMPLETE SENTENCES (INCLUDING ARTICLES SUCH AS A, AN, AND THE)

Cutlines should be written in complete grammatical sentences. The telegraphic style of headlines, in which articles and other words are omitted, is not used in cutlines.

> Five-year-old Suzie Cutie of Falmouth eats an ice cream cone on a bench at Bicentennial Beach.

5. WRITE CUTLINES IN THE PRESENT TENSE

The cutline should describe what is happening in the photograph at the time it was taken. Even though the photograph was taken in the past, the cutline should be written in the present tense. If necessary, the time element can be explained in a separate sentence.

> President Jimmy Carter visits the Three Mile Island Nuclear Power Plant in Middletown, Pa. The photograph was taken during the crisis in 1979.

6. EXPLAIN WHAT IS HAPPENING IN THE PHOTOGRAPH

The best news photographs show action. The best cutlines explain that action. For example, imagine a photograph of a police officer talking to a group of visitors and pointing to his right. The cutline must explain the situation.

> At West Dennis Beach, Officer Lance Leaning tells Loretta King, Bryan Sanders, and Linda Herbert where they can sit to avoid disturbing the nesting area for endangered piping plovers.

7. EVERY PHOTOGRAPH ALSO SHOULD HAVE A CREDIT LINE

People will want to know who took the photograph. This is important for legal and historic reasons, as well as simple information. In some cases the photograph is the property of the photographer; in other cases it is the property of the publication. In either case, that information should be printed clearly near the photograph when it is reproduced. People who want to reprint it will need to find out who owns the copyright, if any, to the photograph. Newspaper and magazine photographs have a way of getting cut out and saved in scrapbooks or other places, and it will be helpful to future generations to know who took the photograph. Furthermore, it is common courtesy to give credit where credit is due.

8. STAND-ALONE PHOTOS (THOSE WITHOUT STORIES) REQUIRE MORE EXPLANATION THAN DO PHOTOS THAT ILLUSTRATE STORIES

Some photographs are printed without accompanying stories. They are called *free-standing art*, *stand-alones*, or *wild art*. Since there is no story to provide background information, it is a good idea to provide more information than usual in the cutline.

9. IN GENERAL, KEEP CUTLINES AS SHORT AS POSSIBLE

Cutlines of photos with stories should be about 10 to 30 words. Cutlines for stand-alone photos should be about 20 to 50 words. These are only rough estimates, and exact lengths depend on the situation. Use enough words to identify everyone in the photograph and explain what they are doing, but no more.

10. DOUBLE-CHECK TO BE SURE THAT THE SUBJECT'S NAME IS SPELLED CORRECTLY IN BOTH THE CUTLINE AND THE STORY

Of course, names must be spelled right in every part of a newspaper, but there is a common problem that shows up in cutline writing. Occasionally, the reporter will interview someone, and a photographer will photograph the same person at a different time. A good copy editor will make sure that the spellings supplied by the reporter and the photographer match. If they don't, more research is needed. All you know is that at least one of them is wrong.

> In February of 1990 I was Sunday editor of the *Cape Cod Times*, and on a Saturday night we received a photograph from the Associated Press showing Nelson Mandela meeting with South African president F. W. deKlerk. It was the first photograph of Mandela distributed in 27 years and signaled his imminent release from prison.
>
> I decided to make it the lead photograph at the top of page one. While the folks in the composing room made the color separations we needed for our production process, I wrote the cutline from memory. It said something like, "Nelson Mandela, left, and South African president F. W. deKlerk meet in Cape Town." It was only after the press began to run that I had the opportunity to see the color photograph and cutline together. Mandela was not on the left; he was on the right!
>
> I immediately told the press foreman to stop the presses. He asked if he should keep the press running while we prepared the corrected page, but I said no, I didn't want a single edition going out with the wrong cutline. It would just look too bad to have deKlerk and Mandela mixed up in what was one of the most historic photographs of the twentieth century.

How to Use Photos and Graphics

1. BE AWARE THAT READERS LOOK AT PHOTOS AND GRAPHICS FIRST

Researchers have used various techniques to watch people as they read newspapers and magazines. The research indicates that people tend to look at photographs and illustrations before they look at text. The implications for journalists are that art can be used to draw people into stories. One good way to do this is to compile a package with elements from top to bottom in the following order: photograph, cutline, headline, and story. In this way, people will start at the top and work their way down the package.

2. WHEN WRITING OR EDITING A STORY, ALWAYS TRY TO THINK OF A PHOTOGRAPH OR A GRAPHIC TO ACCOMPANY IT

A reporter may research and write a story without giving much thought to a photograph or other graphic device to illustrate it. A good editor will step in and suggest a photograph, if appropriate.

3. THE BEST PHOTOGRAPHS SHOW PEOPLE DOING SOMETHING. AVOID PHOTOS OF BUILDINGS OR OF PEOPLE POSING FOR THE CAMERA

Photojournalism is a special kind of photography. Posed or staged photographs are not considered good photojournalism. The best news photographs are taken when the subjects are doing what they would be doing whether or not a photographer were present.

The worst photographs in newspapers are the awkward "grip-and-grin" shots of two people shaking hands and smiling at the camera. Most good newspapers refuse to print such photographs. People holding an award, a plaque, or a check fall into the same category.

Avoid asking someone to pretend to be doing something. Such pictures look staged.

4. WHEN SELECTING PHOTOGRAPHS, MAKE SURE THAT THEY ARE IN SHARP FOCUS AND HAVE HIGH CONTRAST. PHOTOS WITH SOFT FOCUS AND POOR CONTRAST ONLY GET WORSE WHEN REPRODUCED IN A NEWSPAPER

Newspapers are printed on high-speed rotary presses that are fast but do not produce the highest possible reproduction quality. For this reason, poor-quality photographs get even worse when reproduced in newspapers. This is why newspapers look for sharp, clear photographs that will reproduce well.

5. SELECT THE VERY BEST PHOTOGRAPH AVAILABLE, AND MAKE IT THE LEAD PHOTOGRAPH OF THE NEWSPAPER

Just as the best story should be the lead story, the best photograph should be the lead photo. An interesting photograph will attract people to the newspaper and get their attention. Similarly, the best photo available for each page should be the lead photo of the page and should be twice the size of any other artwork on the page.

6. WHEN USING A PHOTOGRAPH, FIRST CROP IT IN TO THE MOST IMPORTANT AREA. THEN ENLARGE THAT PART TO THE BEST SIZE

Sometimes a photograph includes some extraneous space that is not needed. Large areas of blank space do not look good in photographs. Occasionally, some background is needed to give a photograph artistic balance, but in general, a photograph should be cropped to include only the important parts.

7. ONCE YOU HAVE CROPPED A PHOTOGRAPH, YOU HAVE DETERMINED ITS SHAPE, WHICH CANNOT CHANGE. IT CAN BE ENLARGED OR REDUCED, BUT THE SHAPE REMAINS THE SAME

The general principle is that the ratio of the width to the depth remains the same. Because you know the original width and depth, and you can choose how wide to make it, you can determine the reproduction depth.

These calculations can be done with a cropping wheel, a calculator, on paper, and in some graphics programs on a computer, but the principle is always the same.

The formula is: Reproduction width divided by the original width times the original depth equals reproduction depth. Thus, if you have a photo that is 8 by 4 inches and you want it to be 6 inches wide, it will become 6 by 3 inches.

Also remember that there is a limit to changing the size of a photograph. If you enlarge a photograph, you run the risk of making it grainy. If you reduce it too much, you run the risk of making it too small to see the parts clearly. One rough guideline is that faces should be no smaller than a dime. In newsrooms, a photo with lots of tiny faces is jokingly referred to as an "attack of the pinheads."

8. WHEN USING MULTIPLE PHOTOS IN ONE PACKAGE, GROUP THE PHOTOS TOGETHER. GROUPS OF THREE OR FIVE PHOTOS WORK WELL

Photo packages or groupings can be very effective when assembled well. Most experts recommend clustering the photos together rather than scattering them around on a page, mixed with text. Having the photos line up with each other gives the package an orderly look, although there should be variety in their sizes.

For some reason, groups of three or five photos have been found to work well. An odd number of photographs seems to work well. However, using more than seven photos on a page rarely works well.

In the 1940s and 1950s, some editors were fond of overlapping photographs, a technique known as *mortising*. This technique has been largely discredited and is used rarely.

9. GOOD INFORMATIONAL GRAPHICS CAN CONVEY LOTS OF INFORMATION IN A VERY SMALL SPACE

Among the best informational graphics are maps, graphs, and charts. These can give readers a lot of information in less space than would be needed to tell the story in words. Nothing beats a locator map for telling readers where something happened. They are not needed to tell people where Washington, D.C., is, but if a plane crashes in a remote place, a map can locate it instantly. Graphs can convey a trend or pattern instantly, and charts can show the relationships among data.

Graphics should be used to impart information, not to fill space. If a graphic is needed to convey vital information, it improves the story. If it is tossed in just to fill a hole on the page, it probably will detract from the story. Content should be the controlling factor in deciding whether or not to use an informational graphic.

10. OTHER GRAPHIC DEVICES CAN BE USED TO MAKE A PAGE MORE ATTRACTIVE. THESE INCLUDE BOXES, LIFTOUT QUOTES, CAP INITIALS, DROP HEADS AND SUBHEADS, AND "REEFERS"

Computer pagination has made it relatively easy to enhance pages with special features. Boxes are excellent ways to tie together packages that include several different elements. Another use of boxes is to set off a special article that is different from the other elements on the page. Each newspaper or magazine should have its own graphic style and have a general policy about when boxes should be used.

When a few words are pulled from the story and reproduced in a type size that is larger than body type in order to give them special prominence, it is called a *liftout quote, quote-out, read-out, pull quote,* or *breakout.* They are usually packaged with a line above and below, and they are usually also found in the text in normal-size type. The purpose is to attract the reader's attention.

When the first letter of a story is printed in a headline-size type, it is called a *cap initial* or *initial cap.*

When a second, smaller headline follows the main headline, it is called a *drop head.*

When small headlines are inserted periodically throughout the text of a story, they are called *subheads.*

All these devices can add to the visual appeal of a page, but they should be used for a purpose, not scattered randomly.

How to Edit Stories

How one goes about editing a story depends on the situation. The process is different at newspapers, magazines, and other media outlets. Typically, the editing at magazines is much more thorough than at newspapers. The following list is an idealized plan of how the editing process should work.

1. FIRST, READ THE STORY COMPLETELY BEFORE MAKING ANY CHANGES

When you are an editor, it is hard to read a story without changing anything. Unless you are under extreme time constraints, it is worth it to take the time to give the story a first read without touching a thing. This ensures that you know everything in the story before you start changing things.

For example, if you see a term in the second paragraph that needs explanation, you might insert the explanation, only to discover that the explanation was included several paragraphs later. It would be better simply to move it up than to write a new one and later delete the reporter's original explanation.

2. STOP AND THINK ABOUT THE PURPOSE, THEME, OR POINT OF THE STORY. IS IT CLEARLY EXPRESSED IN A LEAD OR IN A "NUT GRAF"?

Once you have gotten through the first read, you should be able to state the main point of the story in one simple sentence. Is that sentence right up there in or near the lead of the story? If the story lacks a "nut graf," you know that is a major problem. If it does have a "nut graf," identifying it will help you determine how to proceed.

3. DECIDE HOW MUCH WORK THE STORY REALLY NEEDS

The decision of how to edit a story depends on how much work it needs. Here are four broad categories:

1. It needs minor editing for spelling, grammar, and style only. In this case, you will be able to proceed immediately to the editing steps with little trouble. Fortunately, most stories will fall into this category.

2. It needs major editing, including rearranging of parts and some rewriting. In this case, the editor will reorganize it into a logical order and rewrite awkward parts, making sure, for example, that every person is identified properly on first reference, since the order of references to people may have changed.

3. It needs rewriting by the editor to present the same information more clearly. If at all possible, the revised version should be checked by the reporter to make sure that it still reflects the reporter's impression of what happened. The more changes an editor makes, the more important it is to work with the reporter. A major change in the lead always should be checked by the reporter.

4. It needs to be rewritten by the reporter. Some stories cannot or should not be rescued by an editor. They must be sent back to the reporter for a complete rewrite. If fixing the story requires additional reporting or a change in focus, that work should be done by the reporter, not the editor. In this situation, the editor should be very clear about what is wrong with the story, including its strengths and weaknesses.

In cases 2 through 4, it is a good idea to make a copy of the original story so that it can be compared with the revised version later.

4. AFTER ANY REORGANIZING OR REWRITING, READ THE STORY A SECOND TIME FOR CONTENT

Having determined how much work the story needs and rewriting if necessary, go through it a second time, paying particular attention to content issues. Make sure that there is a clear lead or "nut graf" and that all parts of the story follow that lead. Make sure that each paragraph logically follows the one before it. Make sure that there are no libelous statements in the story. Look out for unattributed statements, missing information, or unclear sentences. If you have doubts about the accuracy of minor details in a story and they cannot be easily verified, delete them.

5. READ THROUGH THE WHOLE STORY CHECKING ONLY THE SPELLING

Go through the story a third time looking at each word to make sure that it is spelled correctly. Do not rely on a computer spell checker (see Chapter 12). Be especially careful with names and titles. Make sure that each name is spelled consistently each time that it comes up. Check agreement with AP style.

6. READ THROUGH A FOURTH TIME LOOKING FOR GRAMMAR AND PUNCTUATION

The fourth read is a good time to double-check the grammar of the story. Make sure that there are no run-on sentences or verb-agreement problems. Look at every comma to make sure that it is used correctly. Look at every pronoun to make sure that its antecedent is clear. Be careful of the most common errors, such as *its/it's* and *there/their* (see Chapter 8).

7. AFTER FOUR READS, YOU ARE READY TO WRITE A HEADLINE

It should be easy to summarize the story in four to eight words. Look at the summary lead or the "nut graf," and simplify it into a headline (see Chapter 29). If you have trouble writing a headline, the story may not have a clear enough focus.

8. IN GENERAL, EDIT LIGHTLY

Fix things that are clearly wrong, but do not change a reporter's writing just because you would have phrased something differently. Allow the individual voices of different reporters to come out. The finished story should sound like the reporter's voice, not the editor's voice.

9. WHEN DEALING WITH THE REPORTER, BE DIPLOMATIC

Good stories result from cooperation and teamwork, not confrontation. If you are working as an editor and you need some information from the reporter to improve the story, it always helps to thank the reporter for working with you and to compliment the reporter on the strong parts of the story. Then you can point out the weaknesses and express a desire to work together to improve the finished product.

10. IF THE STORY IS NOT GOOD ENOUGH, DO NOT USE IT

Stories with fatal flaws should be killed or sent back to the reporter for a total rewrite. Publishing a story with serious errors is never a good idea. But be sure that you have a good reason to kill a story; do not reject an article just because you don't care for the writing style or the subject.

Legal Considerations in Journalism

*M*edia law is the study of the laws and legal precedents that apply to the mass media. This chapter gives a very brief oversimplification of a few issues in media law; it is not intended to provide legal advice. Journalists with specific questions should consult an attorney specializing in media law for guidance on specific situations. Most news media keep lawyers on retainer for just such situations.

1. THE MOST FUNDAMENTAL LAW OF JOURNALISM IN THE UNITED STATES IS "CONGRESS SHALL MAKE NO LAW ... ABRIDGING THE FREEDOM ... OF THE PRESS"

The First Amendment to the Constitution of the United States says, "Congress shall make no law respecting an establishment of religion, or prohibiting the free exercise thereof; or abridging the freedom of speech, or of the press; or the right of the people peaceably to assemble, and to petition the government for a redress of grievances."

Prior to the American Revolution, many people (including Ben Franklin's older brother James Franklin) had been jailed for printing things that upset government leaders. The founding fathers wanted to be sure that would never happen in the United States, so "the freedom of the press" is enshrined in the First Amendment. This is why no government body can pass a law saying that everything in a newspaper must be true.

Radio and television stations that broadcast over the air are subject to the regulations of the Federal Communications Commission (FCC) and do not enjoy the freedom of printed media. Courts have ruled that "the freedom of the press" does not include broadcast media, although the general principles of freedom of speech and freedom of expression prohibit the government from being too restrictive.

2. RECENT COURT DECISIONS HAVE GRANTED FULL FIRST AMENDMENT PROTECTION TO THE INTERNET

Although it is an emerging field of media law, American courts have given wide protection to statements on the Internet. Other countries (most notably China) have been much more restrictive.

According to David L. Hudson Jr. of the First Amendment Center, "the U.S. Supreme Court in *Reno v. ACLU* (1997) noted . . . that the Internet is entitled to the highest level of First Amendment protection, akin to the print medium."

3. THERE ARE VERY FEW LEGAL RESTRICTIONS ON NEWSPAPERS AND MAGAZINES UNDER CRIMINAL LAW, BUT JOURNALISTS CAN BE SUED UNDER CIVIL LAW

The area where journalists are in most legal jeopardy is under civil law, which refers to lawsuits brought by individuals rather than the government. Under civil law, people can sue each other if they feel that they have been harmed. Sometimes people sue journalists when they feel that a news story harmed them.

4. THE MOST IMPORTANT LEGAL ISSUE FOR JOURNALISTS IS LIBEL LAW

Reporters, editors, and publishers can be forced to pay damages to plaintiffs if found guilty of libel. Libel is essentially a false and defamatory statement that is published. Courts have held that for a journalist to be guilty of libel, the statement must have caused harm to the plaintiff, it must be false, and it must have been published.

A common example of libel is when an article damages someone's reputation with a specific falsehood. The person must be clearly identified, and the false accusation must be reasonably specific. Just saying someone is "stupid" or "ugly," for example, is not specific enough to cause a successful libel action. But calling a doctor a "quack" or calling anyone a "pedophile" certainly would be cause for a libel suit.

5. THE SUPREME COURT CASE NEW YORK TIMES V. SULLIVAN MADE IT MORE DIFFICULT FOR PUBLIC FIGURES TO COLLECT DAMAGES IN LIBEL CASES

The Supreme Court has ruled that freedom of the press is essential for the success of American democracy. In some cases, even a statement that is false and defamatory must be allowed. In the 1964 landmark case, *New York Times v. Sullivan,* the court ruled that "debate on public issues should be uninhibited, robust, and wide-open and that it may well include vehement, caustic, and sometimes unpleasantly sharp attacks on public officials."

The New York Times had published a full-page advertisement placed by civil rights leaders supporting the work of the Rev. Dr. Martin Luther King Jr. The ad was signed by many prominent Americans, including former First Lady Eleanor Roosevelt. It was critical of Alabama police officials. One police commissioner, Louis Sullivan, sued *The New York Times* and demonstrated that there were errors in the advertisement. The Alabama Supreme Court found the *Times* guilty of libel. But the *Times* appealed to the U.S. Supreme Court, which overturned the state court decision on the grounds that the lower court decision would put too much of a damper on debate about important public issues.

The Court said that newspapers should not be punished for making reasonable errors in such a situation as criticizing a public official unless the public official could prove "actual malice." In this situation, they said, "actual malice" would be to publish something the newspaper knew to be false or to show reckless disregard for the truth.

Private citizens are not required to prove actual malice to win libel suits because robust examination of their actions is not as vital to a democracy.

6. TRUTH IS A DEFENSE IN LIBEL CASES

In any libel suit, whether by a public official or a private citizen, truth is a defense. If the plaintiff cannot prove the statement is false, there is no libel. The most important way for journalists to avoid libel suits is to make sure that everything they print is true.

7. THE RIGHT OF FAIR COMMENT PROTECTS REVIEWERS FROM LIBEL SUITS

Journalists are also protected from libel suits if they are reviewing a public performance and making comments about the quality of that performance. The most famous case in the history of the principle of fair comment is the 1901 *Cherry Sisters* case before the Iowa Supreme Court.

The Cherry Sisters were a singing trio who were famously bad. According to contemporary reports, their audiences routinely threw rotten vegetables at them. After an appearance in Odebolt, Iowa, *Odebolt Chronicle* editor William Hamilton wrote:

"Effie is an old jade of 50 summers, Jessie a frisky filly of 40, and Addie, the flower of the family, a capering monstrosity of 35. Their long, skinny arms, equipped with talons at the extremities, swung mechanically, and soon were waved frantically at the suffering audience. The mouths of their rancid features opened like caverns and sounds like the wailings of damned souls issued therefrom. . . . Effie is spavined, Addie is stringhalt, and Jessie, the only one who showed her stockings, has legs without calves, as classic in their outlines as the curves of a broom handle."

The Cherry Sisters sued for libel. The Iowa Supreme Court ruled that: "One who goes upon the stage to exhibit himself to the public, or who gives any kind of a performance to which the public is invited, may be freely criticized. . . . The comments, however, must be based on truth . . . and the matter must be pertinent to the conduct that is made the subject of criticism. . . . Surely, if one makes himself ridiculous in his public performances, he may be ridiculed by those whose duty or right it is to inform the public regarding the character of the performance."

8. CERTAIN STATEMENTS ARE "PRIVILEGED," WHICH PROTECTS JOURNALISTS FROM LIBEL SUITS

Besides truth and fair comment, a third area of protection for journalists is the law of privileged statements. Courts have ruled that journalists cannot be found guilty of libel for reprinting accurately testimony made in court, statements made on the floor of a legislative body, and certain official documents, including police reports. The importance of free and unfettered reporting of these documents outweighs any harm done if the statements contained therein turn out to be false and defamatory.

9. THE WORD ALLEGEDLY IS NO PROTECTION AT ALL IN A LIBEL SUIT

If an allegation is made, it is the duty of the reporter to say who is making the allegation. If the police have charged someone, it should be reported that way. The word *allegedly* will do nothing whatsoever to protect a reporter in a libel suit.

10. PEOPLE ARE ENTITLED TO A REASONABLE EXPECTATION OF PRIVACY

The right of privacy is not stated explicitly in the Constitution, but courts have held repeatedly that Americans do have such a right. Occasionally, people sue journalists for invading their privacy. The general guideline used by journalists to avoid losing a privacy suit is this: If a person does something or says something in plain view of the general public, it is safe to photograph or report on that activity. If, for example, a man says or does something, and you can see him while standing on a public street, then he cannot win a suit against you for reporting what he said or did.

> In 2003, a former journalism student came to my office in tears. Her sister's family had been victimized twice. First they lost their home to a fire; then they lost their privacy to a newspaper photographer. She wanted my advice.
>
> Fortunately, the family was able to escape unharmed. But they lost their home and all their possessions. Two days after the fire, my former student's young nieces were unable to comprehend the enormity of the situation. One of the girls was sitting at her grandmother's kitchen table eating cereal, and she looked at the local newspaper open in front of her. There, on a page of local news, was a black-and-white photograph of the charred remains of a room in her house with her favorite stuffed bear blackened from the blaze. It was devastating for the young child.
>
> My former student was outraged. How could the newspaper get away with that? Couldn't they sue the newspaper?
>
> I said, yes, they could always sue the newspaper, but they probably would lose the lawsuit. The court probably would rule that the public had a right to know about major news events in town, and the house fire was newsworthy. It turns out that the photographer had not entered the house but had walked around the outside of the house accompanied by firefighters. He got the poignant shot by shooting through a window that the firefighters had broken open.
>
> Was that an invasion of privacy? It certainly was from the family's point of view. I urged my former student—who was an excellent writer—to write a letter to the editor criticizing the newspaper. I said she could say in the letter that the family felt it was an invasion of privacy and that the family felt it had been victimized twice. I said she had a better chance of winning the case in the court of public opinion than in a court of law.

Ethical Considerations in Journalism

*M*edia ethics is the study of the moral principles and roles of conduct that apply to those who practice journalism, which is the occupation of reporting, writing, editing, photographing, broadcasting, or otherwise presenting news.

1. THERE IS A BIG DIFFERENCE BETWEEN WHAT IS LEGAL AND WHAT IS ETHICAL

Because of the freedom of the press enshrined in the First Amendment, newspapers and magazines in the United States are legally entitled to print almost anything. It is legal to print stories saying that the president is consulting with spacemen from Mars. It is legal to print pornographic pictures of adults engaged in bizarre sexual activities. It is legal to print a story saying water is bad for people. But is it *ethical?* This is a different question altogether, and one that is much more difficult to answer.

2. MEDIA ETHICS ARE TWO PLURAL WORDS

Media is the plural of *medium.* A *medium* is an intermediate substance that carries something, such as information, from a source to a receiver. *The New York Times* is one medium. *Hustler* is another. A teenager's Web site devoted to news about a rock 'n' roll band is a third. When people talk about a "vast media conspiracy," as if the media were one thing, they are missing a very important point. The mass media is not one thing; they are thousands of different things controlled by thousands of different people. At the beginning of the twenty-first century it is true that a few large corporations have bought up many of the most popular mass-media outlets, but there are still thousands of others not under the control of those corporations. Even those that are owned by a big corporation frequently exercise a great deal of autonomy in editorial matters.

Some linguists have begun to accept the idea that *media* can be construed as a singular collective noun, but honoring its original definition as the plural of *medium* helps to foster a better understanding of the diversity of the mass media in American society today.

Ethics is the plural of *ethic.* An *ethic* is a moral principle of conduct. "Thou shalt not kill" is an ethic. "Clean up your own mess" is another. Sometimes we try to develop whole systems to be a guideline for right conduct, and we call those *ethics* or *codes of ethics.*

However, in America today it would be hard to come up with any one set of ethics with which we would all agree. Even "Thou shalt not kill" is interpreted different ways by different people. Some believe that we must avoid killing even disease-carrying mosquitoes or property-destroying termites. Others believe that it is acceptable to kill people if they are enemies or deserters in time of war or to kill criminals who commit certain crimes.

In media ethics, there are similar questions. Is it acceptable to print the name of a juvenile accused of a crime? Is it acceptable to print the name of a victim of rape? Is it acceptable to print a picture of a woman who purposely exposes her breasts in public? What if it happened by accident? Different publications would answer those ethical questions differently.

3. THERE IS NO ONE CODE OF ETHICS FOR ALL JOURNALISTS

The Society of Professional Journalists has a code of ethics. So does the American Society of Newspaper Editors (ASNE), the National Press Photographers Association, the Radio-Television News Directors Association, the Society of American Business Editors and Writers, The Associated Press, *The New York Times,* the *Los Angeles Times,* the *Washington Post,* and Dow Jones, Inc., publisher of the *Wall Street Journal.* They are all accessible through the Web site of ASNE. They are all different.

In general, they stress the importance of acting responsibly to inform the public accurately and fairly while preserving freedom of the press.

4. JOURNALISTS SHOULD AVOID CONFLICTS OF INTERESTS

Most journalists agree that news writers should not report on areas in which they have financial interests. If a reporter, for example, owned a restaurant, it would be unethical for that reporter to write a restaurant review or a news story about that restaurant. Perhaps the reporter would be tempted to slant the coverage to make the restaurant look better than it is. Even if the reporter could resist that temptation, the readers—if they found out about the connection—would suspect the accuracy of the coverage. So reporters have to avoid the appearance of a conflict of interest.

Less obvious conflicts come up more frequently. Should a reporter who owns a boat cover a meeting about expanding his or her marina? Should a reporter who received a free dinner cover the after-dinner speech? Should a sportswriter who received free admission to a game, courtesy of the home team, cover that game? Responsible people may have different answers to such questions.

5. ACCEPTING GIFTS RAISES ETHICAL ISSUES FOR JOURNALISTS

Because journalists have the "power of the press," people frequently try to curry their favor by offering them gifts. Although small tokens of appreciation generally are accepted as posing no ethical problems, expensive gifts generally are regarded as unacceptable. The credibility of a newspaper or broadcast news operation suffers if people learn that reporters are accepting valuable gifts.

For several years I worked as a travel editor for a daily newspaper that had a modest travel section every Sunday. About once a week I received invitations to participate in familiarization tours in which groups of travel editors would visit a resort area with all expenses paid by the area's travel and tourism office, chamber of commerce or the businesses themselves.

I received offers for all-expense-paid trips to China, to Australia, and to Disney World, among other places. Each time I explained that our newspaper's policy prohibited me from accepting any gifts of value. Probably the hardest one to give up was the annual call from a woman with a sultry voice inviting me to a resort spa in Florida. She offered me free food, transportation and accommodations, including "a free aromatherapy massage." I am not even sure what that is, but it always sounded like the best offer I ever refused.

6. THE USE OF OFF-THE-RECORD INFORMATION RAISES SERIOUS ETHICAL ISSUES

David Shaw, media critic at the *Los Angeles Times,* began a column in July 2003 with the following statement: "I can think of no common journalistic shortcoming more threatening to media credibility than over-reliance on unnamed sources. Polls consistently show that people object to—and are skeptical of—'sources said' stories. Almost invariably, they say, they assume that any quote without a name attached to it was made up by the reporter."

A few excellent stories have relied on unnamed sources—the reporting of Bob Woodward and Carl Bernstein for the *Washington Post* about the Watergate scandal won a Pulitzer Prize despite its heavy reliance on unnamed sources.

However, most stories do not require a reporter to promise to keep secrets. Reporters are in the business of spreading information, not keeping secrets. When they agree to go "off the record," it puts them in an awkward situation. In some cases (depending partly on varying state laws), a judge can compel a reporter to reveal a source. Many reporters have been jailed for contempt of court for refusing to reveal a source.

Most editors advise reporters to use anonymous sources only in the rarest circumstances when no alternative exists. Most journalists find that if you refuse to go "off the record" and tell your source you will only use the information if you can use his or her name, the source will give you permission to do so.

There also can be confusion about the exact meaning of various terms, such as *off the record, not for attribution, background,* and *deep background.* If you have to use any of those terms, make sure that all parties involved agree on what you mean. Be sure that all such ground rules are clear before the interview begins.

7. SOMETIMES REPORTING CAN MAKE THE JOURNALIST PART OF THE PROBLEM

Scientists conducting experiments always attempt to make sure that their actions do not affect the outcome of the experiment. Similarly, journalists should be careful that they do not exacerbate a problem by the process of their reporting on it. It is generally considered acceptable for a journalist to bring a problem to light, thereby facilitating its solution, but most people agree that journalists should not become part of the story.

For example, psychologists say that some teenagers can be encouraged to commit suicide if they hear that several of their peers have done so. For this reason, many editors decline to report news of suicides in order to avoid encouraging others to imitate that behavior. Bomb threats (where there is no real bomb) generally also are not reported in order to avoid encouraging copycats.

There are many ethical questions involved in deciding whether something is newsworthy. If a handful of noisy demonstrators create a scene, should the media report on their activities, even though their point of view may be rejected by the vast majority of residents? Or does that only serve their purpose and give them more credibility than they deserve? Would it matter if they were from a group most people find offensive, such as the Ku Klux Klan or a neo-Nazi group, or if they were from a more respected group, such as Mothers Against Drunk Driving or parents protesting school budget cuts?

8. THE RIGHTS OF A FREE PRESS CAN CONFLICT WITH THE RIGHTS TO A FAIR TRIAL

Volumes have been written about the problem of the conflict between the people's right to have a free press and the people's right to have a fair trial. In countries without a free press, some trials are held in secret, and people can be shipped off to jail without anyone knowing what happened. In the United States, however, the news media are allowed to cover criminal proceedings from arrest through sentencing, holding the whole process up to public scrutiny.

However, the publicity surrounding some crimes can make it difficult to select an impartial jury. Sometimes judges have closed courtrooms to the press or issued gag orders prohibiting participants from talking to the press. In other cases, trials have been moved to other locations, where there wasn't as much publicity.

Responsible journalists strive to inform the public as completely as possible while always remembering that a person accused of a crime remains innocent until proven guilty.

9. NOTIONS OF GOOD TASTE, PROFANITY, OBSCENITY, AND PORNOGRAPHY VARY WIDELY

Some words and pictures always have been acceptable to almost everybody, and other words and pictures have been offensive to almost everybody. In between them lies a constantly changing landscape of shifting sands. What is in poor taste depends on the time, place, and publication.

Most daily newspapers that circulate to the public in the United States try to avoid printing words that you would not use in front of your elderly grandmother or your impressionable little boy because either of them may read the paper.

So-called men's magazines, on the other hand, have no such restrictions. Other magazines with a more serious literary reputation, such as the *Atlantic Monthly* or the *New Yorker*, occasionally will print profanities in a context of serious literary merit. Many European newspapers print photographs of bare-breasted models to boost circulation.

In 1980, President Jimmy Carter reacted to a primary challenge by Sen. Edward M. Kennedy by saying, "I'll whip his ass." It was a newsworthy quote, but many American newspapers feared it was too offensive for their readers, so they printed it as, ". . . whip his a¨"." About that same time, many newspapers would not carry advertising for or even print any mention of condoms. In 1984, however, Surgeon General C. Everett Koop mailed a pamphlet to every household in America explaining the importance of using condoms to prevent AIDS. After that, most newspapers used the word freely.

But it was another nine years before the word *penis* became common in newspapers, largely as a result of the celebrated case of John and Lorena Bobbit. Papers found it too difficult to explain what Mrs. Bobbit cut off her husband without using the word *penis*. Not long thereafter, *vagina* found its way into the popular press when newspapers began reporting on the off-Broadway show "The Vagina Monologues" in 1996. However, few general-circulation newspapers will print the vulgar slang terms for those organs.

Each media outlet tries to determine what is acceptable to its readers or viewers, and a responsible news writer will be aware of those policies.

10. IN DECIDING WHETHER OR NOT SOMETHING IS ETHICAL, IT MAY HELP TO ASK YOURSELF IF YOU COULD JUSTIFY IT TO SOMEONE WHOSE RESPECT YOU TREASURE

Ethics is usually considered a branch of philosophy, not psychology. But a psychological approach helps many people to decide on a course of action. Before taking an action, ask yourself if you could justify it to your daughter, your grandfather, or a respected mentor. Picture your innocent young child asking you why you put that picture on the front page. If you have an answer that makes you feel comfortable, go ahead and print it. If you find yourself squirming, perhaps there are ethical issues that you need to consider.

11. A GOOD JOURNALIST SHOULD STRIVE TO "DO NO HARM"

Most scholars believe that it was Hippocrates in his book *The Epidemics* who first advised doctors "to help, or at least do no harm." This is a good rule for journalists, too. Most editors would agree that there are times when printing something that is truthful and newsworthy might cause more harm than good.

If a group of people were arrested for making a harmful drug out of common household ingredients, few newspapers would print the recipe. There are times when the White House press corps agrees to withhold details of the president's schedule for security reasons because printing them would do more harm than good. If a battered woman is taken to a safe place for protection, few responsible journalists would publish the location, even if they knew it.

What makes this particularly difficult is that journalists often are unaware of unintentional harm a story may cause. It is useful, when possible, to take a few minutes to consider whether a story might have unintended consequences.

> In 1995 the Cape Cod Times published an award-winning series of articles exposing the epidemic of domestic violence plaguing Cape Cod. The series documented the large number of women who were beaten by their husbands or boyfriends, and the fact that most local police departments were not taking the problem seriously enough. The series also included useful information for victims, including telephone numbers of places where victims could seek help. As a result of the series, every police department in the area reexamined its way of handling domestic-violence calls. Each one appointed a domestic-violence officer or task force. I was proud of being one of the lead editors on the series.

After the series ended, we continued to print follow-up articles on the subject. In one of them, reporter Mark Merchant and photographer Vincent DeWitt got permission from the Yarmouth, Mass., police department to ride along with officers responding to domestic violence calls. One evening, the Yarmouth Police went to enforce a restraining order against an abusive ex-boyfriend. The woman wanted the police to remove all the man's belongings from the house, where she lived with her three young children. When they arrived at the house, the officers explained that a reporter and photographer were with them and asked if it was all right if the journalists observed the procedure. The woman said it was OK. She gave the journalists permission to tell her family's story, use their names, and take their pictures.

When he got back to the newsroom, Vince told me he thought he had gotten a hell of a shot—one that perfectly demonstrated the human toll of domestic violence. When I saw it, I agreed. "Are you sure you got permission to take that?" I asked. Both Vince and Mark assured me that the woman had given her permission.

The photograph was dramatic. In the foreground was a uniformed police officer carefully carrying two shotguns through the dining room. In the background was the woman's 7-year-old daughter, sitting at the dining room table with both hands over her mouth. The officer had a stern expression on his face, the little girl looked terrified. The story explained that the little girl had been sitting at the table making a card with crayons. It read: "To the police, thank you."

I made it the lead photo at the top of page one of the Sunday paper.

Soon the letters started coming in. One said the picture "displayed gross insensitivity to the child." The letter asked, "What were you thinking by using a child to sensationalize and sell papers?" I felt terrible.

Then another letter came in. It said, "The expression on the little girl's face as she watches a policeman carry away the guns will not easily be forgotten. . . . Somehow, somewhere it should be displayed so that we will keep in mind what a long way we have to go to reach a happy and civilized society." I felt great.

Then I got a call at my desk. The receptionist said there was an irate woman in the lobby who wanted to know who was responsible for putting that picture in the Sunday paper. That would be me.

It was the little girl's mother. She said that when she gave permission for the reporter and photographer to cover her story, she had no idea what that photograph would look like in the Sunday paper. She had no idea how much it would upset the little girl, who was now afraid to leave the house or go to school. She also pointed out that her boyfriend had been verbally abusive, but that he had never threatened them with his shotguns, which he only used for hunting. The photograph gave the wrong impression, and it traumatized her daughter. She cried.

I apologized to the woman and said I had not intended to do any harm. I wrote a note to the little girl apologizing to her and urging her to return to school. A few days later I got a telephone call from the little girl in the picture, and she told me she was feeling better and going to school again. After that I cried. I asked the woman if there was anything I could do to make up for her troubles. She said she had an idea that someone should use one of Cape Cod's abandoned farms as a place where people on welfare could work to grow their own food and sell the extra they produce to help them get back on their feet and off welfare. She wondered if we could publish a story about her idea. We did that, and a few years later a similar idea was taken up by a local agency with the resources to make it happen.

You can never be sure how your decisions as a news writer or editor will affect people.

(NOTE: A video version of this anecdote that shows the photograph mentioned is available on YouTube.com, and can be located by searching for the author's name.)

The Future of the Mass Media

1. THE REPORTS OF THE DEMISE OF JOURNALISM ARE PREMATURE

With newspapers folding and budgets shrinking, some wonder if there is any future for journalism. The unequivocal answer is: Yes, there is.

The first decade of the twenty-first century was an extremely difficult one for journalism in general and especially difficult for the newspaper industry. A few major newspapers ceased publication and those that remained saw revenues shrink. The primary causes were the worldwide recession, the shift of classified advertising to free online sites (primarily Craigslist), and a shift in most people's reading habits away from newspapers to the Internet.

The recession is part of an economic cycle that was already rebounding in 2010, and many newspapers and media companies were already reporting improved economic situations. Classified advertising is not likely to return, but newspapers are beginning to focus on other revenue sources and benefit from decreased expenses that had been associated with classified advertising, including newsprint and personnel. As for the third factor, the shift in reading habits, the change appears to be a slight decrease in newspaper reading, rather than a wholesale abandonment of the medium. The death of newspapers was predicted with the invention of newsreels, radio, and television, and the current death watch is likely to be equally premature.

What seems lost likely is that the basics of journalism and the basics of news writing will continue well into the future. Since the dawn of humanity, people have wanted to know what is going on. People have always longed for a timely account of a recent, interesting, and significant event. There will always be a demand for people who have the talent, skill, and experience to provide that service. These news stories will be presented through a variety of media, including some that have not yet been invented, but the old-fashioned basics—such as "who, what, where, when, why, and how"—will remain in demand.

During the recession years from 2008 to 1010, it became apparent that newspapers were in a period of transition to a new economic model. There are many different ideas of how that will turn out, but there were some hopeful signs.

2. NONPROFIT JOURNALISM ENTERPRISES MAY SIGNAL A NEW ECONOMIC MODEL FOR JOURNALISM

One major development was the birth of nonprofit journalism groups, such as ProPublica, which won a Pulitzer Prize for investigative journalism in 2010. According to its Web site (www.propublica.org), "ProPublica is an independent, non-profit newsroom that produces investigative journalism in the public interest. Our work focuses exclusively on truly important stories, stories with 'moral force.' We do this by producing journalism that shines a light on exploitation of the weak by the strong and on the failures of those with power to vindicate the trust placed in them."

The work of ProPublica is supported entirely by donations, and all its work is published on its Web site and also offered to traditional newspapers and other news media.

Similar effort in the San Francisco Bay Area is called "Spot.Us." According to its Web site (http://www.spot.us/):

"Spot.Us is a nonprofit project of the "Center for Media Change" and funded by various groups like the Knight Foundation. We partner with various organizations including the Annenberg School of Communications in Los Angeles. We are an open source project to pioneer "community powered reporting." Through Spot.Us the public can commission and participate with journalists to do reporting on important and perhaps overlooked topics. Contributions are tax deductible and we partner with news organizations to distribute content under appropriate licenses. On some occasions we can even pay back the original contributors."

Meanwhile National Public Radio and The Public Broadcast Service have been providing nonprofit journalism in the broadcast field for decades.

3. TRADITIONAL NEWSPAPERS CAN STILL MAKE MONEY

Nonprofit models offer exciting new possibilities, but it is still possible for traditional newspapers to turn a profit. To cite one example, *The New York Times* reported a profit in 2009 after suffering losses in the previous few years. The New York Times Company, which, in addition to its flagship "gray lady," publishes the *Boston Globe* and 16 other daily newspapers, reported an annual profit of $19.9 million in 2009. Hundreds of smaller community newspapers have continued to be profitable, even through the recession years.

According to the Newspaper Association of America, nearly 100 million adults continue to read a print newspaper every day. Millions of others, who get their news from Web sites like Google News or Yahoo.com, are reading news stories originally written for print newspapers of the Associated Press.

Clearly we are in a period of transition to new business models and new forms of presentation, but as long as people want to know what is going on in the world, there will be a demand for good journalists who understand the elements of news writing.

4. SO FAR, EVERY TYPE OF MASS MEDIA HAS CONTINUED TO EXIST AFTER NEW ONES WERE INVENTED

Books were the first means of communication that were able to reach vast audiences. The book industry is considered the first mass medium. Pamphlets, broadsides, and other printed matter also emerged soon after Gutenberg's printing press popularized printing in Europe in the 1400s. The printing press also made possible newspapers and magazines, generally considered the second and third mass media. All of these media existed concurrently. More significantly, they are all vibrant and popular today.

When radio emerged as a mass medium in the 1920s, many thought it would replace newspapers, and when television emerged in the 1950s, many thought it would replace radio and newspapers, at least as a source for news. So far the older media have changed with the times and made way for the new media, but they have not disappeared.

At the beginning of the twenty-first century, many people were predicting the death of newspapers. Arthur Sulzberger, Jr., publisher of *The New York Times,* was quoted in the Israeli newspaper *Haatez* in 2007 as saying, "I really don't know if we will be printing the *Times* in five years, and you know what? I don't care either."

As newspaper profits have declined from approximately 30 percent return on investment to about 20 percent, corporate owners have grown concerned and ordered staff reductions, but the profit margins remain higher than in most other businesses.

It seems premature to write the obituary for newspapers. As the famous newspaper reporter, essayist, and novelist Mark Twain once said, "The reports of my death have been greatly exaggerated."

5. MEDIA CONVERGENCE IS AN IMPORTANT TREND, AS OLD MAINSTREAM MEDIA SUCH AS NEWSPAPERS TRANSFORM THEMSELVES INTO INFORMATION SUPPLIERS USING A VARIETY OF EMERGING MEDIA

Most newspaper companies, including *The New York Times,* have expanded into multimedia operations with Web sites, blogs, streaming videos, and places for readers to contribute their information and views. Most newspaper reporters are now expected to contribute audio and video reports as well as written stories, and many write blogs and interact with readers over the Internet. Radio and television news reporters also participate in this convergence journalism by putting their work on the Internet.

Other media, not usually associated with news reporting—such as recorded music and the movies—are also a part of this media convergence as films and recordings establish Web sites and interact with their audiences. The 2006 film *Snakes on a Plane* was rewritten before its release based on suggestions fans posted on the film's Web site.

6. THE MASS MEDIA TEND TO UNDERGO "DE-MASSIFICATION," AS THEY TRY TO APPEAL TO A SPECIFIC AUDIENCE

A trend that has been particularly strong since the 1950s is the tendency of media to select content to appeal to a specific audience. Radio stations design music play lists to appeal to a specific demographic audience. Magazines emerge to serve either general audiences in a geographic region, such as *Yankee* magazine, or national audiences of people interested in a specific activity, such as *Runners World.* The largest national newspapers, including the *Wall Street Journal, USA Today, The New York Times,* and the *Washington Post,* have seen their circulations level off or decline at the beginning of the twenty-first century. Many smaller regional and local newspapers did have increases in circulation, another indication of de-massification of the mass media.

7. DIGITALIZATION OF INFORMATION HAS AFFECTED EVERY ASPECT OF THE MASS MEDIA, AND THIS TREND IS LIKELY TO CONTINUE

The conversion of data into binary forms began as early as World War II, but became more widespread in the 1970s. With the explosion of personal computers and the development of the World Wide Web in the early 1990s, amazing quantities of information became available to anyone with a computer and an Internet connection.

One effect of this digitalization of information is that journalists can easily access background information for news stories. Looking up previously published stories used to be a matter of leafing through yellowed newsprint clippings in a newspaper's "morgue." Now the same task can be accomplished in far less time with a computer.

Information compiled by reporters that is available in digital form is much easier for readers, viewers, and other journalists to access. Besides the obvious advantages, this also means that plagiarism, copyright violation, and other forms of theft of intellectual property are also much easier. Once material is on the Internet, it is virtually impossible to control its use and redistribution.

8. THE INTERNET IS LIKELY TO BECOME NOT A MASS MEDIUM IN ITSELF, BUT A BROAD PLATFORM THAT CAN HOST MANY DIFFERENT MASS MEDIA

In 2010 most lists of the mass media included books, newspapers, magazines, recorded music, motion pictures, radio, television, and the Internet. (Some include secondary mass media, such as billboards, posters and other signs, and perhaps pamphlets, brochures, and mass mailings.) The newest of the major mass media—the Internet—is still evolving. As more and more people gain access to the Internet, there is no question that it reaches a mass audience. A more important question is whether it is one mass medium or a platform that can support various media.

Before the emergence of the World Wide Web in the early 1990s, the Internet hosted bulletin board pages. These evolved into Web pages on the World Wide Web. Since then, several different kinds of media have emerged on the Internet. There are chat rooms and discussion groups. Interactive multiplayer games allow many people to interact with an artificial environment.

Blogs are Web logs set up to make it easy for people to post periodic updates on any subject they choose. At the National Writers Workshop in Hartford, Conn., in March of 2007, Denis Horgan of MSNBC estimated that there were 70,000 bloggers and 70,000 blog readers, for an average readership of one person per blog. But a few very popular blogs have thousands of regular readers. Most newspapers and many television and radio stations have reporters blogging on the Internet. Are blogs a mass medium?

Another possible medium is the alternate-reality worlds emerging on the Internet. Sites such as Second Life allow users to establish characters and communicate with other characters. There are ways to communicate with thousands of other people in these worlds. Should those methods be considered mass media or, perhaps, virtual mass media? Social networking sites, such as MySpace, Linkedin, and Facebook, allow people to create their own Web pages and interact with others who have similar pages. The remarkable growth of Facebook in 2009 and 2010 drew a great deal of attention to that site and also raised concerns about privacy. Are these social networking sites a mass medium?

9. THE STRUGGLE TO CONTROL INFORMATION WILL CONTINUE AS NEW MASS MEDIA EMERGE

Just as the kings and queens of fifteenth century Europe tried to control printing presses, people who have power in the twenty-first century are attempting to control the newest media. Dictatorial regimes limit access to the Internet in their countries. In the Western democracies it is more likely to be corporate business interests trying to control information. In 2010 and 2011, a debate was being played out over whether Internet Service Providers should be allowed to control the speed at which various sites on the World Wide Web were delivered to their customers. Companies that deliver the Internet to cable subscribers, for example, might want to encourage users to use Internet services from the same company and discourage customers from using services of their competitors. In December 2010 the FCC issued new regulations limiting how Internet Service Providers could restrict their customers' access to the Internet, a policy known as "Net Neutrality."

Meanwhile debates over censorship of "adult," "pornographic," or "obscene" materials are bound to continue. This type of material has proved to be one of the most popular uses of the Internet. The Federal Communications Commission, which regulates broadcast material on radio and television, has not been involved in regulating the Internet, but some people believe it should be.

10. CELL PHONES OR SIMILAR PORTABLE PERSONAL COMMUNICATION DEVICES WILL PLAY A MAJOR ROLE IN THE EMERGENCE OF NEW MASS MEDIA IN THE TWENTY-FIRST CENTURY

Cell phones have revolutionized the way reporters gather news, and may soon revolutionize the way consumers receive news. Until the 1990s few reporters had any kind of portable communication devices. Press conferences or other news events often ended with reporters scrambling to be the first at a nearby pay telephone. These days, a reporter would not consider covering an event without a cell phone. The Iraq war is covered by reporters sending live satellite phone reports as events happen.

It is unclear at this point whether the use of cell phones, or similar portable communication devices, will be considered a mass medium itself or whether these devices will simply provide access to various mass media. The introduction of the iPhone by Apple in 2007 popularized the idea that a cell phone could also be a way to access the Internet, including e-mail, GPS navigational information, recorded music, and other features. The BlackBerry, with many of the same features, had already become popular five years earlier. Emerging technology to extend wireless Internet connectivity to more and more areas is bound to transform the way people receive news rapidly.

11. SYSTEMS TO CREATE ORDER AND RATIONALITY OUT OF THE INFORMATION OVERLOAD WILL BE HIGHLY VALUED IN THE TWENTY-FIRST CENTURY

With millions of Web sites, blogs, personal sites, and other digital stops on the "Information Superhighway," access to information is seemingly unlimited. People need a good method to find their way through the maze of information overload. Sites such as Google News and the home pages of traditional news outlets are trying to establish themselves as places where people can stop for a sampling of the most important news. This is the role traditionally played by editors at newspapers or news directors at broadcast media. Because of digitalization of information, the Internet raises the possibility that news sites can be customized for the individual preferences of the consumer. Whether this is desirable or valuable is another question.

12. THE BASIC PRINCIPLES OF NEWS WRITING WILL CONTINUE TO BE AS IMPORTANT IN THE WORLD OF BLOGS AND PODCASTS AS THEY WERE IN THE EARLY DAYS OF NEWSPAPERS

In 1919, William Strunk, Jr., wrote in *The Elements of Style,* "Omit needless words." Those words will be even more important in 2019. Our global civilization is buried in excessive verbiage. As more and more information is made available to people, the demand to have it presented in a clear, concise, and accurate form will be greater than ever.

13. THE NEED FOR JOURNALISTS WILL CONTINUE

Who will provide a timely account of recent, significant, and interesting events? Thanks to the Internet, anyone can post information that everyone can read. But not all of it is timely. Not all of it is significant. Not all of it is interesting. Furthermore, not all of it is accurate.

It is likely that people will tend to return to news sources where they find the stories are timely, significant, interesting, and accurate. The ability to create stories that have those qualities is not an easy job. It is the job of a journalist. It is the craft of news writing. People who are able to do that well will remain in demand. They may be posting their stories in a variety of formats on a variety of media that are yet to be developed, but people who can tell a good story have been in demand since prehistoric days, and the emergence of new forms of mass communication is unlikely to change that.

In the spring of 2007 I attended a workshop at Middlesex Community College in Bedford, Mass. One of the speakers was Jim Campanini, editor of the Sun of Lowell, Mass. He showed us how his newspaper was integrating audiovisual presentations such as slide shows and video clips on its Web site. He said they were using the Web site to interact with readers and tell stories that could not be told as well in the old-fashioned print way. He said he would never hire another reporter who couldn't shoot video.

"Aha!" I said to myself. "I have seen the future of journalism."

The next speaker was Steve Kurkjian, investigative reporter for the *Boston Globe.* He talked about how only print reporters could take the time to do real investigative reporting and present complicated stories in all their complexity the way they should be told. The tangled web of sexual abuse by Roman Catholic priests is an example of the kind of story that can't be told in a 15-second video clip. It needed to be told in long stories in print.

"He's right," I said to myself. "Newspapers can do important investigations. If people want video, they can watch TV."

Are old-fashioned print newspapers a thing of the past? I think I found my answer—maybe yes, maybe no.

Tips from the Best

1. "Write the things which thou hast seen, and the things which are, and the things which shall be hereafter."
—Revelations 1:19, The Holy Bible.

2. "Read over your compositions, and, when you meet a passage which you think is particularly fine, strike it out."
—Samuel Johnson (1709–1784), English author, critic, and lexicographer, author of the *Dictionary of the English Language* and the 10-volume *Lives of the Poets.*

3. "The difference between the right word and the nearly right word is the same as that between lightning and lightning bug."
—Mark Twain (Samuel L. Clemens) (1835–1910), American journalist, humorist, and author of *Huckleberry Finn* and *The Adventures of Tom Sawyer.*

4. "Put it before them briefly so they will read it, clearly so they will appreciate it, picturesquely so they will remember it, and above all, accurately so they will be guided by its light."
—Joseph Pulitzer (1847–1911), American publisher, editor, and journalist who was born in Hungary and moved to the United States as a young man and created one of the nation's largest publishing empires.

5. "Omit needless words." . . . "Vigorous writing is concise. A sentence should contain no unnecessary words, a paragraph no unnecessary sentences, for the same reason that a drawing should have no unnecessary lines and a machine no unnecessary parts. This requires not that a writer make all his sentences short, or that he avoid all detail and treat his subjects only in outline, but that every word tell."

—William Strunk, Jr. (1869–1946), American literary critic and writing educator. These quotes are from his classic writing manual, *The Elements of Style*, which was first published in 1918 and revised by E. B. White in 1959.

6. "To write simply is as difficult as to be good."

—W. Somerset Maugham (1874–1965), English author who was born in and lived part of his life in France. Among his best-known works are *Of Human Bondage, The Moon and Sixpence,* and *The Razor's Edge.*

7. "I write a little every day, without hope and without despair."

—Isak Dinesen (Karen Blixen) (1885–1962), Danish author and essayist, author of *Out of Africa.*

8. "I consider that that 'that' that worries us so much should be forgotten. Rats desert a sinking ship. Thats infest a sinking magazine."

—James Thurber (1894–1961), American author, cartoonist, humorist, and satirist. This quote is from a memo he wrote to an editor at the *New Yorker* magazine, which published much of his work.

9. "Never use a metaphor, simile or other figure of speech which you are used to seeing in print. Never use a long word when a short word will do. If it is possible to cut a word out, always cut it out. Never use the passive when you can use the active. Never use a foreign phrase, a scientific word, or a jargon word if you can think of an everyday English equivalent. Break any of these rules sooner than say anything outright barbarous."

—George Orwell (Eric Arthur Blair) (1903–1950), English author, satirist, essayist, and reformer. He is the author of the great political novels *1984* and *Animal Farm.* This quote is from his essay "Politics and the English Language."

10. "Dealing with the media is more difficult than bathing a leper."

—Mother Teresa (Agnes Gonxha Bojaxhiu) (1910–1997), Roman Catholic nun, humanitarian, winner of the Nobel Peace Prize in 1979.

11. "Clutter is the disease of American writing. We are a society strangling in unnecessary words. . . . Fighting clutter is like fighting weeds—the writer is always slightly behind."

—William Zinsser (1922–), American journalist, editor, author, and teacher. This quote is from his book *On Writing Well.*

12. "Prefer the short word to the long. Prefer the familiar to the fancy. Prefer the specific to the abstract. Use no more words than necessary to make your meaning clear."

—Rene J. Cappon (1924–), American journalist and editor. Originally from Vienna, Austria, he moved to New York as a youth and worked for the Associated Press for more than 30 years. This quote is from his writing guide, *The Word*, which was revised and republished as *The Associated Press Guide to News Writing.*

13. "You expect far too much of a first sentence. Think of it as analogous to a good country breakfast: what we want is something simple, but nourishing to the imagination. Hold the philosophy, hold the adjectives, just give us a plain subject and verb and perhaps a wholesome, nonfattening adverb or two."

—Larry McMurtry (1936–), American novelist, author of *Lonesome Dove* and *Terms of Endearment.*

14. "Most rock journalism is people who can't write, interviewing people who can't talk, for people who can't read."

—Frank Zappa (1940–1993), iconoclastic American singer, songwriter, musician, and author of *The Real Frank Zappa Book.*

15. "I don't so much mind that newspapers are dying. It's watching them commit suicide that pisses me off."

—Molly Ivins (1944–2007), political columnist, editor, author, and humorist.

16. "Being a reporter is as much a diagnosis as a job description."

—Anna Quindlen (1953–), Pulitzer Prize-winning columnist for *The New York Times* and *Newsweek* and author of novels, nonfiction books, and children's stories.

INDEX